Joyce LaFray's *Underwater Gourmet*

A Famous Florida!® Cookbook

Seaside
Publishing, Inc.

oyce LaFray's *Underwater Gourmet*

Joyce LaFray's Underwater Gourmet
A Famous Florida!® Cookbook
Published by

Publishing, Inc.

P.O. Box 14441
St. Petersburg, FL 33733

Visit our Website at: famousflorida.com
E-mail: sales@famousflorida.com

Manufactured in the United States of America
ISBN: 0-942084-55-1
Library of Congress Catalog Number: 00 092696
Copyright ©2001 by Joyce LaFray

Senior Editor: Vicki Krueger
Cover and book design by: Aaron Grudis and Joanne Smout
Illustrations by: Jack Emmert and Tim Foley
Many thanks to the restaurant owners, managers, and chefs who
contributed their favorite recipes to this book.

Dear Seafood Lover:

Ever since I moved to Florida in 1975, I have been a lover of fish, shellfish, and many underwater delights. It's easy here in Florida, where my back yard is the magnificent Gulf of Mexico.

For twentysome years, I have had the pleasure of sampling nearly every type of fresh seafood available, cooked in a myriad of ways. The result of this lengthy adventure lies within the pages of this newly revised and edited Underwater Gourmet.

For each recipe included, a dozen more could have been, that is, if time and space were allowed. The choices within the pages of this book were based on my travels throughout the state, along with rec-ommendations from many: food editors, salespersons, locals, tourists, taxi drivers, visiting celebrities, and many others. Criteria? Great and memorable taste.

I know that you will enjoy these recipes with as much gusto as I have. This book has been in print for two decades, and the recipes and stories have been updated to make it even better. I think you will find it to be a most comprehensive collection, and I am anxious to get your response.

So, get ready, you're about to embark on a very special Underwater tour!

Warm regards,

Joyce LaFray

Joyce LaFray

Notes from the Test Kitchen

I collected a variety of recipes from restaurants throughout our Sunshine State and then, with my associates, tested each and every one of them in our Test Kitchens. Some did not test easily, so they were not included in this book. If they didn't work in the test kitchen, they would not work for you.

Here are some suggestions for you as you enjoy preparing these recipes:

- Before marketing and planning your meal, read each recipe over carefully to eliminate surprises. One of these recipes needs to marinate for 30 days!

- Some varieties of fish are difficult to find fresh. Have an open mind and allow for substitutes when you shop. Also, find a good fish market whose staff can give you good advice about what's best to buy when. They can be a tremendous help in fish cookery.

- Unless otherwise indicated, all the ingredients listed in these recipes should be the freshest you can find. You may substitute frozen, but it won't taste as good!

- Use lightly salted butter unless otherwise specified and extra virgin olive oil when ever possible. It's healthful and contains no cholesterol.

- Cooking and preparation times are approximate. Everyone works at a different speed; stoves heat differently; and even cooking pans and utensils affect timing.

Dedication

This book is dedicated to my wonderful, supportive,
loving, and remarkable husband,

Henry Edward Little

FAMOUS
florida!®

PENSACOLA
PANAMA CITY
TALLAHASSEE
JACKSONVILLE
ORANGE PARK
GAINESVILLE
ST. AUGUSTINE
CEDAR KEY
DAYTONA BEACH
OCALA
HOMOSASSA SPRINGS
ALTAMONTE SPRINGS
TARPON SPRINGS
TAMPA
ORLANDO
CLEARWATER
AUBURNDALE
ST. PETERSBURG
LAKE WALES
PALMETTO
FORT PIERCE
SARASOTA
PALM BEACH
BOYNTON BEACH
CAPTIVA ISLAND
FORT MYERS
DEERFIELD BEACH
FORT LAUDERDALE
NAPLES
MARCO ISLAND
MIAMI
KEY WEST
ISLAMORADA

Table of Contents

MULLET MAMA

Saltwater Fin Fish

Fans of Fish

Seafood lovers can rejoice—one of their favorite foods is not only delicious, it's nutritious. Seafood has been proven to be a rich source of protein and vitamins, and is lower in fat and cholesterol than beef and pork.

Seafood is also an excellent source of omega-3 fats. These polyunsaturated fatty acids (the building blocks of fats) can help lower the type of fat that contributes to heart disease. Omega-3's also make red blood cells more flexible so they flow more smoothly. Other health problems, such as asthma, diabetes, migraine headaches, and some kidney disease, may be controlled or alleviated when you eat omega-3's. As a bonus, fish are one of the most important sources of calcium.

Fat and Lean Fish

Before you start cooking, be aware of the different fat levels found in fish. The fat content of most varieties of fin fish is less than five percent; some are less than one percent. The amount of fat depends on the species, the season, and even the water depth where the fish are found.

In general fat fish:

- have more oil in the flesh
- have darker flesh
- have a stronger flavor
- are well-suited for broiling or baking
- need little extra fat or liquid to stay moist

Lean fish:

- have oil concentrated in the liver
- have a more delicate flavor
- go well with sauces
- need basting when broiled or baked
- maintain quality during freezing

Getting Fresh

Before you select your fish, check out the market. The store should smell of salt and ice. If it smells less than fresh, be careful. That "fishy" smell develops over time and means some fish have been around too long.

If your market passes the nose test, it's time to get personal. When you buy fresh whole fish, look them over first. The fish should be bright and shiny, with most of the scales still sticking to the skin. The eyes should be clear and bright; they might even protrude. Eyes will turn pink or cloudy when fish get stale. When you press the fish with your finger, the meat should spring back. Most important, fresh fish should smell fresh and like the sea.

Fish fillets and steaks should look fresh-cut, with no browning or drying around the edges. If they're packed, they should be tightly wrapped, with little or no air space and no liquid.

Whole fish may come un-gutted, or drawn. Its entrails and sometimes the gills have been removed. Dressed fish have been drawn and had the scales removed. Pan-dressed fish have had the head, tails, and fins removed.

On Ice

Frozen fish should be frozen all the way through. They should be wrapped tightly and should have no odor. If you see ice crystals or water stains, the fish may have thawed at some point. Fish that's been thawed and re-frozen reduces the quality of texture and flavor. Any white, dark, or dry spots mean the fish has been damaged through drying or it has freezer burn. If there's an expiration date, check it before you buy it. Frozen fish will keep for up to six months; sometimes longer.

To freeze your fish, wash all the blood and excess slime from the body cavity. Never freeze un-gutted fish; the entrails decay much more rapidly than the meat. Freeze quickly at 0° F. or below in small, airtight packages. To help prevent freezer burn and rancidity, freeze fish in water in waxed cartons, freezer bags, or other containers.

Another freezing process is called "glazing". Package and freeze the fish until solid. Remove from the freezer, unpack the fish, and dip it into ice cold water. Re-pack it and put it back in the freezer. The fish will be covered with a glaze of ice, which will further protect the flavor.

Temperature's Rising

Never thaw fish at room temperature. Place it in the refrigerator from 18 to 24 hours, or place under cold running water.

Best Buys

Make sure you get the most economical cut of fish before you buy it. The following chart shows the edible percentage of fish in its various forms. For example, if the price per pound of fillets is no more than 55 percent more than the price of whole fish, it is more economical to buy the fillets. If the fillets are no more than 50 percent more than the price of drawn fish, fillets are the better buy.

Fillets: 100 percent

Steaks: 86 percent

Dressed: 67 percent

Drawn: 46 percent

Whole: 45 percent

As a rule of thumb, two pounds of fillets will serve six people, three pounds of dressed fish will serve six, and six whole fish will serve six diners.

From Market to Table

Before cooking, wash the fish thoroughly, dunk it well in salted water, and quickly dry it inside and out. Lay fillets on paper towels and turn once or twice to dry.

All fish are tender before they are cooked. Cooking develops the flavor and acts as a coagulant. Stick a fork in the fish to see if it's done. Perfectly cooked fish is nearly opaque (except for tuna and salmon), and it should be moist. It should easily flake (separate or fall easily into its natural divisions) when it's done. If it's dry, it's overdone.

Cooking time varies with the thickness and size of the fish. Test it, at the thickest point, about halfway through cooking, and then frequently until it is done.

Remember:

Pan frying Best for fillets, fish sticks, or small fish.

Sautéing Best for fillets, steaks, larger fish cut into cubes.

Baking Fine for all types of fish.

Broiling Fine for almost all types of fish except smaller ones.

Steaming Fine for almost all types of fish.

Poaching Fine for almost all types of fish.

Planking Best for whole dressed fish, or fish steaks.

Fat Content for a Selection of Saltwater Fish

Fat (6% to 20% or more)

Albacore
Bonito
Dogfish
Halibut (Greenland)
Herring
Mackerel (Atlantic and Spanish)
Mullet, Striped
Pompano
Sablefish
Salmon (Pacific, Atlantic, Chinook, Coho, Red, Sockeye)
Sardines (Atlantic, Pacific)
Shad
Smelt
Spot
Sturgeon
Trout, Rainbow (Steelhead)
Whitefish

Intermediate (2% to 6%)

Alewife
Barracuda
Bass, Striped
Bluefish (Skipjack, Snapping Mackerel)
Butterfish (Gulf)
Croaker (Atlantic)
Herring (Pacific)
Jack Mackerel
Kingfish (Whiting)
Porgy
Sheepshead
Smelt
Swordfish

Trout, Brook (Atlantic)
Tuna, Bluefin (Horse Mackerel, Horse Tuna, Albacore)
Tuna, Bonito
Tuna, Yellowfin (Yellowtail, Tunny)
Weakfish (Shad, Trout, Sea Trout)
Whiting (Kingfish)
Weakfish
Yellowtail

Lean (Less than 2%)

Bass, Sea
Cod
Croaker, White, Yellowfin (Pacific), Drum (Atlantic)
Flatfish (Winter Flounder, Fluke, Sole)
Grouper
Hake (Whiting)
Haddock
Halibut
Lingcod (Pacific)
Ocean Perch
Pike, Walleye
Pollack
Rockfish
Sea Trout
Snapper
Sturgeon
Sucker, White
Tautog (Blackfish, Chub, Oysterfish, Black Porgy, Moll)
Tilefish
Tomcod

La Reserve's Grouper Sauce Vierge

Ah, how well I remember well the magnificent fresh fish dinner I enjoyed at this long-gone Fort Lauderdale restaurant! It is not vital for sauce ingredients to marinate for two days, but longer marination does intensify the flavors. Top the fish with chopped parsley, and serve lemon wedges on the side.

GROUPER

4 6- to 8-ounce grouper fillets
1/2 red onion, chopped
3/2 cup dry white wine
1/2 peeled carrot, sliced
1 to 2 crushed bay leaves
4 sprigs fresh parsley
Lemon slices for garnish

1. Add all the ingredients, except the grouper, to a large pot. Add enough water so that the grouper will be covered, and simmer for 5 minutes.

2. Add grouper and poach for 8 to 10 minutes or until done.

3. Remove the grouper and serve with the Sauce Vierge.

SAUCE VIERGE

5 to 6 tomatoes, peeled, seeded, and chopped
1/5 bunch parsley, chopped
2 lemons, halved and thinly sliced
3 black peppercorns
3 tablespoons extra virgin olive oil
1/3 clove garlic, skin intact and smashed
Salt and pepper to taste
2 to 3 fresh basil leaves, or 1 teaspoon dried

1. Combine all of the ingredients and marinate in the refrigerator for 1 to 2 days.

SERVES: 4
PREPARATION TIME: 30 MINUTES
COOKING TIME: 10 MINUTES
MARINATE: 1 TO 2 DAYS

LA RESERVE, FORT LAUDERDALE

Le Petite Fleur's Grouper Niçoise

The remarkable combination of delicious imported olives, anchovy fillets, and red ripe tomatoes with fresh fish is a sure-fire ticket to heaven.

2 pounds grouper fillets, or any other firm, white fish
Salt and white pepper to taste
Worcestershire sauce
Lemon juice
Anchovy oil, or may use anchovy paste
6 tablespoons extra virgin olive oil
4 cloves garlic, chopped
6 imported black ripe olives, pitted and sliced
8 green pitted olives, sliced
4 large ripe tomatoes, peeled, seeded, chopped
3 anchovy fillets
¹/₂ cup fish stock*
¹/₂ cup dry white wine such as Chardonnay
Chopped, fresh parsley

1. Preheat oven to 350° F.

2. Rinse grouper and pat dry. Season with salt, white pepper, Worcestershire sauce, lemon juice, and anchovy oil.

3. In a medium-hot, oven-proof sauté pan, sauté the grouper in olive oil.

4. Turn over and place in oven until almost done (keep juicy and do not over cook).

5. Remove fish from pan and drain off oil.

6. To the same pan, add garlic and olives. Deglaze* with white wine and fish stock.

7. Add chopped fresh tomatoes and chopped anchovy fillets.

8. Put fish on top of mixture and let simmer for 2 minutes or until the fish is cooked.

9. Place fish on plate, cover with the Niçoise garnish and sprinkle with chopped parsley.

* SEE GLOSSARY

SERVES: 4
PREPARATION TIME: 10 MINUTES
COOKING TIME: 10 MINUTES

LE PETITE FLEUR, TAMPA

Siple's Baked Grouper Piquante

Dick Siple, one of Clearwater's pioneers in the culinary scene, brought a touch of class to the area in his cozy garden-like restaurant. In place of grouper, use snapper, sole, or haddock with equally successful results.

1 pound grouper fillets or other firm, white fish
2 tablespoons fresh lemon or lime juice
Extra virgin olive oil
1 tablespoon or more of Dijon mustard
Coarse dry bread crumbs
Melted butter or extra virgin olive oil
12 cups water
Fresh chopped parsley for garnish

1. Preheat the oven to 400° F. Place the fillets, skin side down, in a flat, buttered baking dish.

2. Sprinkle the fillets with lemon juice. Rub on a bit of extra virgin olive oil, then spread the mustard evenly over the fish. Sprinkle the bread crumbs over the fish, then drizzle with the melted butter. Do not moisten heavily.

3. Add a little water to the pan. Bake for 12 to 18 minutes at 325° F. Cooking time will depend on the thickness of the fish and the number of portions. Garnish with fresh parsley.

SERVES: 2 TO 4
PREPARATION TIME: 10 MINUTES
COOKING TIME: 12 TO 18 MINUTES

SIPLE'S GARDEN SEAT, CLEARWATER

The Lobster Pot's Stuffed Grouper Bouquetierre

When you visit Tampa Bay, you may want to dine Gulfside. If this is the case, the Lobster Pot on Redington Shores is always a great choice. If you prefer, rent a kitchenette on the Gulf and prepare this dish yourself. The restaurant used black grouper, but red grouper or any firm, white fish will do just fine.

1 3-to 4-pound grouper, scaled, cleaned and trimmed
Juice of 1/2 lemon
1 teaspoon Worcestershire sauce
Salt and fresh ground pepper to taste
3 cups plain bread croutons, crispy
1/4 cup finely diced celery
1 tablespoon finely diced onions
1/2 cup hot milk; 2 percent or whole
1/4 cup melted butter or extra virgin olive oil
Dash of nutmeg
Hungarian paprika to taste
1 tablespoon fresh thyme, or 1/2 teaspoon thyme
2 cups dry white wine such as Chardonnay

BOUQUETIERRE
2 celery stalks cut in 3-inch pieces
2 peeled carrots, cut in julienne*
1 mild green bell pepper
1 large ripe tomato, peeled and quartered
Flowerets of 1/2 bunch broccoli

* SEE GLOSSARY

CONTINUED...

1. Preheat oven to 400° F.

2. Have fish filleted, leaving head and tail intact. Marinate in lemon juice, Worcestershire sauce, and salt.

3. To make stuffing, mix croutons, celery, onions, hot milk, 2 tablespoons melted butter or extra virgin olive oil, salt, pepper, and nutmeg. Let stand for a few minutes, but do not make a paste. Put stuffing between fillets. Sprinkle generously with paprika.

4. Place in baking pan. Pour remaining butter over fish. Sprinkle with thyme, salt, and pepper. Arrange vegetables around stuffed fish. Add wine and cover tightly with foil.

5. Bake for 35 minutes, or until fish flakes.

SERVES: 2
PREPARATION TIME: 15 MINUTES PLUS TIME FOR STUFFING TO STAND
COOKING TIME: 35 MINUTES

THE LOBSTER POT, REDINGTON SHORES

Selena's Grouper Florentine

This is one of the most spectacular fish dishes in Florida. The mellowness of the creamy, flavorful cheese along with the flavor of the spinach will make your guests love you forever. Try real Vermont Cabot® cheddar for a real treat.

1¹/₂ pounds frozen spinach, defrosted, well drained
1 onion, chopped
Salt and cracked black pepper to taste
1 cup dry sherry
2 pounds grouper fillets
3 cloves garlic, chopped
¹/₄ pound butter or extra virgin olive oil
¹/₄ pound medium sharp cheddar cheese, grated

1. Preheat oven to 350° F.
2. Combine spinach, onion, salt, and cracked black pepper to taste, and sherry. Place in the bottom of a large baking dish.
3. Place grouper on top of spinach. Season with salt, pepper, garlic, and dot with butter or extra virgin olive oil. Put in oven until 90 percent cooked.
4. Remove from oven then and top with cheddar cheese sauce and grated cheese.
5. Place back into the oven until the cheese is melted.

CHEESE SAUCE
¹/₂ pound butter
1 cup all-purpose flour
4 cups milk, whole or 2 percent
¹/₂ teaspoon salt, or to taste
1 teaspoon white pepper
2 cups grated cheddar cheese
4 ounces sherry

1. Melt butter. Slowly add flour and stir constantly to make a roux*. Slowly add milk and whisk until smooth.
2. Add salt, pepper, and cheese. Stir gently until cheese is melted.
3. Cook over low heat for about 10 minutes, or until sauce is thick. Stir in sherry.

* SEE GLOSSARY

SERVES: 6
PREPARATION TIME: 20 MINUTES
COOKING TIME: 30 MINUTES

SELENA'S, TAMPA

Bon Appetit's Grouper Rockefeller

Henri-Louis Pernod, a physician and pharmacist, acquired the recipe for Pernod while he was living in Switzerland. Luckily for us, Henri realized that the lovely taste of anisette is worth working toward.

1 pound spinach, thoroughly washed and stemmed
1¹/₂ cups clarified butter*
¹/₄ cup finely chopped onions
Salt, pepper, and nutmeg to taste
¹/₂ cup heavy cream, or may use lighter version
3 pounds fresh grouper fillets or other firm, white fish
Juice of 2 lemons or limes
Flour for dusting fillets
2 ounces Pernod liqueur
1 cup hollandaise sauce*
Parsley sprigs for garnish
Paprika for sprinkling

1. Preheat oven to 350° F.

2. Blanch* spinach in boiling water for 30 seconds. Drain well; chop fine.

3. In a skillet, cook onions in ¹/₂ cup clarified butter* until onions are soft. Add spinach, salt, pepper, and nutmeg. Mix well and stir in cream. Cook until sauce starts to thicken. Set aside and keep warm.

4. Prepare hollandaise sauce* according to Glossary directions (see page 270). Season grouper with lemon juice, salt, and pepper, then dust with flour.

5. Heat 1 cup of the butter in a hot sauté pan. Add grouper and cook until golden brown on one side. Turn and finish in oven until just done.

6. To serve, place ¹/₆ spinach mixture on each plate. Top with a fillet of grouper. Splash with Pernod and nap* with hollandaise sauce. Garnish with parsley and a dash of paprika.

* SEE GLOSSARY

SERVES: 6
PREPARATION TIME: 20 MINUTES
COOKING TIME: 30 MINUTES

BON APPETIT, DUNEDIN

Cap's Grouper Parmesan

Here's another innovative and delicious dish for our native grouper. Unless you are a true purist, use a low-fat sour cream. It's easier on the waistline.

4 pounds grouper, cut into 6 to 8 pieces
1/4 cup fresh lemon or lime juice
2 pints sour cream
1 cup chopped Spanish onion
1/4 cup Worcestershire sauce
1/4 cup dry sherry
1/8 cup grated Parmesan cheese
1/8 cup fresh chopped parsley

1. Bake fish at 350° F. in a lightly greased baking pan. This will take about 15 minutes.

2. While fish is cooking, mix the remaining ingredients together for the sauce.

3. In an oven-proof dish or baking pan, spread a thin coat of the sauce on the bottom. Place the fish over the sauce and pour the rest of the sauce over the fish.

4. Return to the oven just until sauce is heated through, about 5 minutes.

SERVES: 6
PREPARATION TIME: 10 MINUTES
COOKING TIME: APPROXIMATELY 20 MINUTES

CAP'S SEAFOOD, ST. AUGUSTINE

Easy-Fried Grouper

The secret to excellent fried fish is really no big secret at all—the secret is the freshness of the fish and the quality and content of the batter. The heat of the oil is important, too. The Yearling has been closed for many years, but its heritage lingers on.

4 6-ounce fillets grouper or other firm, white fish
1 cup all-purpose flour
1 cup low-fat milk
1 cup cracker meal
Vegetable or extra virgin olive oil for deep frying

1. Cut grouper into strips about 1 inch wide. Dip evenly in flour, then milk, and then cracker meal.

2. Heat oil to about 340° F. Fry until golden brown, then blot on paper towels and serve piping hot.

SERVES: 4
PREPARATION TIME: 5 MINUTES
COOKING TIME: 5 TO 10 MINUTES

THE YEARLING RESTAURANT, CROSS CREEK

Bon Appetit's Grouper Royale

If there is a dessert among entrées, this is it! Complete the picture with a crisp salad and a bottle of soft white wine.

3 pounds fresher grouper fillets, enough for 6 persons
3/4 pound sweet butter or extra virgin olive oil (at room temperature)
1/2 light brown sugar
1/2 cup finely ground pecans
Juice of 2 lemons or limes
Salt and white pepper to taste
1/2 cup all-purpose flour for dusting
1 1/2 cups clarified butter*
Parsley for garnish

1. Combine butter or extra virgin olive oil, brown sugar, and pecans. Mix until well blended. Set aside.

2. Season grouper with lemon juice, salt, and cracked black pepper to taste. Dust lightly with flour.

3. Carefully pour clarified butter* or extra virgin olive oil and grouper in a hot sauté pan. Cook until fish is golden brown on one side. Turn the fillets. Cover and finish cooking on low heat.

4. Remove fish to a warm platter. Pour off excess fat and add pecan butter to the pan. When batter begins to foam, pour over fillets. Sprinkle with parsley and serve immediately.

* SEE GLOSSARY

SERVES: 6
PREPARATION TIME: 10 MINUTES
COOKING TIME: 20 MINUTES

BON APPETIT, DUNEDIN

Baked Stuffed Grouper en Croûte With Saffron Sauce

The chef at this popular St. Augustine eatery, The Raintree, suggested serving the fresh fish with boiled new potatoes (the smallest are the most delectable!) and fresh broccoli or asparagus. It's a dish fit for a king or queen – and well worth the trouble!

SAFFRON SAUCE

Extra virgin olive oil or butter mixed with extra virgin olive oil for sautéing
1 onion, coarsely chopped
1 peeled carrot, coarsely chopped
1 head celery, coarsely chopped
Head and bones of fish for stock
5 quarts water
2 cups dry white wine
2 tablespoons fresh chopped parsley
1/4 pound unsalted butter
2 cups heavy cream, or lighter version
1 pinch saffron

1. In a large (8- to 10-quart) heavy-based pan, heat a little extra virgin olive oil or butter. Add the onions, carrots, and celery and sauté until slightly softened, about 5 minutes. Add the fish heads and bones. Cover the pan tightly and cook over a medium heat until the fish "sweats"*, about 10 minutes.

2. Remove the lid. Add the water, wine, and parsley and bring to a boil. Reduce the heat and simmer for 30 minutes, skimming the top often.

3. Strain the stock through a colander and then again through a fine sieve. Return to the pot and bring to a boil and second time. Boil briskly until stock is reduced* to about 1 quart.

4. Lower the heat and add the butter in small pieces. Stir in the cream and the saffron, cooking until the sauce is rich and shiny. Adjust the seasoning.

STUFFING

1/2 pound Alaskan king crab, snow crab, or crab substitute
1 pound bay or sea scallops
2 cups heavy cream, or lighter version
1 teaspoon fresh chopped fennel

* SEE GLOSSARY

CONTINUED...

1. Pick over crab for cartilage; discard waste. While stock is reducing, combine the crab, scallops, cream, and fennel in the container of a food processor. Blend until rich and smooth, about 1 minute. Adjust the seasoning.

2. Refrigerate for 20 minutes.

GROUPER

2 pounds fresh grouper (4 very thin fillets, 8 ounces apiece, washed, trimmed and boned)
1 egg, beaten
4 sheets puff pastry** (10" X 7")
Extra virgin olive oil for cooking

1. Preheat the oven to 400° F.

2. While the stuffing is chilling, prepare the fillets. Wash and trim the fish carefully of all skin and small bones. Cut into 4 equal pieces. With a sharp knife, make an incision almost through each piece so that you can open the meat out like an envelope for stuffing. Or, you can slice the fillets thinly so that they can be wrapped around the stuffing.

3. Place the stuffing between each piece of fish, or, if you used the second procedure, place the stuffing on top of the fillet. Close carefully, pressing gently with the fingers.

4. Lay each piece of stuffed fillet on a sheet of pastry, and carefully bring up each of the 4 sides like a small parcel, moistening each edge with beaten egg to make a firm seal. Invert the parcel onto a cookie sheet brushed with oil.

5. Brush the fish parcel with more beaten egg and make a small cut in the top to allow steam to escape.

6. Bake for 20 minutes, or until pastry has risen and is golden brown.

7. To serve, pour a little of the saffron sauce on each plate and place the fish parcel carefully on the sauce. Serve the rest of the sauce at the table.

** AVAILABLE IN THE FROZEN FOOD SECTION, IF NOT PREPARED FRESH.

SERVES: 4
PREPARATION TIME: 30 TO 45 MINUTES
COOKING TIME: 1 HOUR, 20 MINUTES
CHILL: 30 MINUTES

RAINTREE RESTAURANT, ST. AUGUSTINE

Café Chauveron's Fillet of Fish Bermuda

We used Mangrove snapper to test this recipe – delicious. The presentation at Café Chauveron, Florida's most infamous French restaurant, was one of the best ever!

2 tablespoons butter or extra virgin olive oil
6 1/2 pound red snapper fillets
1 cup dry white wine
1 cup fish stock*
2 to 3 shallots, minced
Salt and cracked black pepper to taste
1/2 fresh white or pink Florida grapefruit, peeled and diced
1 32-ounce can pineapple juice
1 bunch seedless red grapes
2 Florida oranges, peeled, pitted, and diced
1 tangerine, peeled, pitted, and diced
1/2 quart heavy cream, or lighter version
3 egg yolks

1. Preheat oven to 475° F.

2. Add butter mixed with a little oil to a heated saucepan. Arrange the fillets over the butter. Add wine, stock, shallots, salt, and cracked black pepper to taste. Cover with well-buttered paper. Bake for about 12 to 20 minutes, depending upon thickness.

3. Remove fish from pan. Arrange it on a preheated platter. Cover the fish with the diced raw fruits: grapefruit, grapes, oranges, and tangerines.

4. Reduce* the juice in the sauté pan a few minutes. Slowly whisk in heavy cream. Stir to blend. Remove from heat.

5. Whip egg yolks and a little cream to blend. Add it to the juice and stir over low heat for 2 minutes or until eggs are warmed through.

6. Pour sauce over the fish and place under broiler until golden brown.

* SEE GLOSSARY

SERVES: 6
PREPARATION TIME: 20 MINUTES
COOKING TIME: 12 TO 25 MINUTES

CAFÉ CHAUVERON, MIAMI

Chateau Parisian's Red Snapper au Pernod

As you may surmise from this cookbook, there is a wonderful affinity between fish and Pernod or anisette. This lovely spirit isn't just for coffee any more.

2 pounds snapper fillets (If you can't locate snapper, any firm white fish works fine.)
3 tablespoons butter, melted
2 shallots, finely diced
1 cup whipped heavy cream
2 ounces Pernod or anisette
Fresh green vegetables such as broccoli, green beans or spinach

1. Preheat oven to 400° F.

2. Cut the snapper into 4 equal portions. Place into baking dish and pour melted butter on top. Bake for 15 minutes or until done.

3. In the meantime, sauté shallots in 1 tablespoon of butter until translucent, then add cream and Pernod. Cook for about 10 minutes or until the sauce becomes thick.

4. Serve immediately with sauce on top of the fish, surrounded by fresh green vegetables.

SERVES: 4
PREPARATION TIME: 5 MINUTES
COOKING TIME: 20 MINUTES

CHATEAU PARISIAN, TAMPA

Sautèed Red Snapper à la Disney®

The fillet stays moist and the flavor is delightfully piquant. Try to buy the smallest red snapper and have it filleted for you. Thin slices have the freshest, most delicate flavor.

5 to 6 ounces red snapper fillet
Salt and black cracked pepper to taste
All-purpose flour for dipping
1 large egg, well beaten
3 tablespoons clarified butter*
Juice of ¹/₂ lemon or lime
1 tablespoon chopped parsley
5 drops Worcestershire sauce
Lemon wedge and parsley spray for garnish

1. Preheat oven to 400° F.

2. Season the snapper with salt and cracked black pepper to taste. Dip in flour, then in egg, being careful to coat well.

3. Place clarified butter* in hot skillet. Sauté fish for about 2 minutes on each side. Place in oven and cook for about 5 minutes. Remove fish to warm platter.

4. Place lemon or lime juice, parsley, and Worcestershire sauce in skillet and cook about 2 to 3 minutes.

5. To serve, pour sauce over fish and garnish with lemon wedge and parsley.

* SEE GLOSSARY

SERVES: 1
PREPARATION TIME: 5 MINUTES
COOKING TIME: 10 TO 15 MINUTES

FISHERMAN'S DECK, EMPRESS LILLY RIVERBOAT
WALT DISNEY WORLD VILLAGE AT LAKE BUENA VISTA

Florida Red Snapper Grecian

Even those guests who are not fond of fish will beg for more of this incredibly delicious dish. It's a winner served with pasta that has been buttered and lightly creamed.

2 pounds red snapper fillets, cut into 4 to 6 pieces
1 cup bread crumbs
4 whole lemons or limes
1/4 cup dry white wine
4 ounces extra virgin olive oil
1/2 cup (1 stick) butter
Oregano sprigs or 1 tablespoon dried oregano
Salt and cracked black pepper to taste
Lemon wedges and parsley for garnish

1. Preheat oven to 350° F.

2. Roll snapper fillets in bread crumbs to cover. Place in a buttered oven-proof pan and baste with some of the butter and extra virgin olive oil. Place pan in oven and bake for 5 to 10 minutes, until almost cooked. Remove pan from oven and place under broiler to brown slightly.

3. Squeeze lemon or lime juice over fish. Add rest of oil and butter, dry white wine, oregano, salt, and cracked black pepper to taste. Place on warm serving plate and pour sauce from pan over snapper. Garnish with lemon wedges and parsley. Serve immediately.

SERVES: 4
PREPARATION TIME: 20 MINUTES
COOKING TIME: 15 TO 20 MINUTES

THE RED SNAPPER, DAYTONA BEACH SHORES

La Reserve's Snapper a L'orange

There is hardly a better combination—fresh seafood and fresh citrus. The acidity of the fruit combines beautifully to create a delicious dish. Prepare garnish first as directed.

GARNISH

2 Florida oranges
4 to 5 quarts water for poaching

1. Remove skin and pith from both oranges. Cut the skin from one orange in julienne.* Poach* strips in water for 1 1/2 minutes or until tender.

2. Remove membrane from both oranges and cut into segments. Reserve along with the julienne strips.

WHITE WINE SAUCE

1/8 cup butter, melted
1/4 onion, chopped
6 ounces dry white wine
1 1/2 ounces dry vermouth
1 tablespoon chopped parsley
2 cups fish stock* (or clam broth)
2 tablespoons heavy cream, or lighter version

1. Sauté onions in the melted butter until just soft. Add dry white wine, vermouth, and parsley and reduce* to three-fourths. Add fish stock and let simmer 15 minutes.

2. Add heavy cream. If you are making this sauce well in advance, do not add cream until just before combining with orange sauce.

* SEE GLOSSARY

CONTINUED...

ORANGE SAUCE

1 cup (8 ounces) fresh orange juice
1/2 stick of butter at room temperature
Salt and cracked black pepper to taste

1. Reduce* orange juice for 1 minute. Remove from heat and whisk in a little butter at a time until it is well incorporated.

2. Whisk in heated wine sauce and salt and cracked black pepper to taste. Keep warm over a low heat or double boiler.

FISH AND POACHING LIQUID

1/2 peeled carrot, sliced
6 ounces dry white wine
1/2 Spanish onion, chopped
1 bay leaf, crushed
2 tablespoons chopped parsley
4 6- to 8-ounce snapper fillets

1. Combine carrot, wine, onion, bay leaf, and parsley and cook for 5 minutes.

2. Place fish in same pan and add water and/or some additional wine to cover. Poach for 8 to 10 minutes or until done.

3. Remove from pan. Place on platter and top with julienne* strips, orange segments, and orange sauce. Serve with rice and tomatoes.

* SEE GLOSSARY

SERVES: 4
PREPARATION TIME: 20 MINUTES
COOKING TIME: 45 MINUTES

LA RESERVE, FORT LAUDERDALE

Lincoln's Baked Red Snapper Spanish Style

For garlic lovers. Serve with rice and a green vegetable. Be sure to have some French or Italian bread to mop up the sauce.

6 6- to 10-ounce snapper fillets
Salt and cracked pepper to taste
1 to 2 onions, sliced 1/4 inch thick
1 to 2 green bell peppers, sliced in 1/4-inch thick rounds
2 cloves fresh garlic, peeled and mashed
1 small (14 to 16 ounces) can whole tomatoes in juice, crushed
3/4 cup lemon juice mixed with 3/4 cup orange juice
Paprika for garnish
1/4 cup extra virgin olive oil

1. Preheat oven to 350° F.

2. Arrange fillets in heavy pan and season with salt and cracked black pepper to taste. Place onions and peppers on top of fish. Mix garlic, tomatoes, and lemon juice together and pour over fish.

3. Sprinkle with paprika. Pour on extra virgin olive oil. Bake 20 to 30 minutes or until fish is just done.

SERVES: 6
PREPARATION TIME: 15 MINUTES
COOKING TIME: 20 TO 30 MINUTES

LINCOLN SPANISH RESTAURANT, TAMPA

Bagatelle's Snapper Rangoon

If you don't mind cleaning an extra pan, start the fruit as soon as you turn the fish over. Try to use fresh pineapple as one of the fruits. Rice with toasted almonds and a tropical salad would be a nice accompaniment.

4 6-ounce snapper fillets
Salt and cracked black pepper to taste
3 eggs, beaten
2 cups milk
All-purpose flour for dredging*
1/2 cup butter
4 to 5 tablespoons fresh lime juice
3 cups diced mixed fruit (banana, melon, pineapple, strawberry, and mango)
Chopped parsley

1. Beat egg with milk, dip fish filets into mixture, then dredge fish in flour that has been mixed with salt and cracked black pepper to taste to taste.

2. Melt 2 tablespoons of butter. Sauté fish for a few minutes and then turn over. (The amount of time depends upon the thickness of the fish.) When cooked, remove from heat and keep warm.

3. Melt remaining 3 tablespoons of butter. Add lime juice and fruit and cook, swirling the pan until the fruit is heated through. The juices will thicken on their own.

4. Pour the juices over the fish and sprinkle with chopped parsley.

* SEE GLOSSARY

SERVES: 1
PREPARATION TIME: 10 MINUTES
COOKING TIME: DEPENDS UPON SIZE OF FISH, NOT MORE THAN 20 MINUTES

BAGATELLE, KEY WEST

Columbia Red Snapper Alicante

Brothers Richard and Casey Gonzmart, and family have kept this recipe in The Columbia Restaurant repertoire for years. Not only will it impress your guests, but also it's easier to prepare than it may seem.

1/2 recipe Columbia Shrimp Supreme (See recipe, page 94)
2 pounds red snapper
2 Spanish onions, sliced
4 cloves garlic, minced
1/2 cup extra virgin olive oil
1 cup dry white wine
3/4 cup brown sauce*
1 pinch of cracked black pepper
1 teaspoon salt, or to taste
4 green bell peppers
8 slices eggplant, breaded and fried
1/4 cup sliced toasted almonds
Parsley sprigs

1. Prepare half of the Shrimp Supreme recipe on page 94.

2. Place snapper on top of onions and garlic in a casserole. Over the fish, pour the extra virgin olive oil, wine, and brown sauce*. Sprinkle with salt and a pinch of pepper, and top with green pepper in slices.

3. Bake in 350° F. oven for 25 minutes or until done.

4. Garnish with eggplant, Shrimp Supreme, almonds, and parsley sprigs.

* SEE GLOSSARY

SERVES: 4
PREPARATION TIME: 10 MINUTES
COOKING TIME: 25 TO 35 MINUTES

THE COLUMBIA RESTAURANTS, TAMPA, ST. PETERSBURG, SARASOTA, ST. AUGUSTINE

Swanson's Fettucine With Smoked Salmon

Leave salmon in long julienne, as it tends to shrink when cooked, and do not overcook. This is a good main course. Canadian smoked salmon is a good substitute, but inventor June Swanson loved the salmon from her homeland.

3/4 **pound Irish smoked salmon, cut in julienne***
1/4 **cup whipping cream**
1/4 **pound butter**
1/4 **cup minced fresh chives**
Fresh ground cracked black pepper
1 pound freshly cooked fettuccine
Parsley sprigs to garnish

1. Combine cream and butter in medium-size saucepan. Cook over medium-high heat until thick, glossy, and reduced* by half. Add salmon, chives, and pepper, and cook, stirring gently, about 1 minute.

2. Transfer fettuccine to serving platter. Pour sauce over and toss just to blend. Garnish with parsley and serve.

* SEE GLOSSARY

SERVES: 4 TO 6
PREPARATION TIME: 15 MINUTES
COOKING TIME: 30 MINUTES

SWANSON'S BISTRO AND WINE BAR, CLEARWATER

Dominique's Potlatch Salmon

Dominique's is no longer on chic Miami Beach, but fond memories linger on when I prepare this favorite of Chef Dominique.

4 8-ounce steaks salmon steaks
1 tablespoon juniper berries (may substitute 1/2 cup gin)
1/4 cup extra virgin olive oil
1 1/2 teaspoons salt
Freshly ground cracked black pepper
Lemon or lime wedges
Hollandaise sauce*

1. Crush juniper berries and sprinkle them over both sides of the salmon steaks, pressing the berries into the meat so they will adhere.**

2. Coat salmon with oil to prevent sticking. Sprinkle with salt and cracked black pepper to taste.

3. Grill over hot coals, 6 minutes on each side, or pan fry in 1/4 cup clarified butter* for approximately the same length of time.

4. Garnish with lemon wedges and serve with hollandaise sauce* or any other sauce of your choice.

* SEE GLOSSARY

**IF YOU CANNOT FIND JUNIPER BERRIES, YOU CAN SUBSTITUTE 1/2 CUP OF GIN. MARINATE THE FISH IN THE GIN FOR A FEW MINUTES.

SERVES: 4
PREPARATION TIME: 10 MINUTES
COOKING TIME: 12 MINUTES

DOMINIQUE'S, MIAMI BEACH, WASHINGTON, D.C.

Café Chauveron's Salmon Mousse With Fennel Sauce

A light, flavorful concoction from my friend André Chauveron. Serve either as a main course or reduce the portions and use as an appetizer.

1¹/₄ pounds fillet of salmon, cut in bite size
1 cup fish stock*
4 egg whites
1 cup heavy cream
¹/₄ teaspoon salt
1 teaspoon black pepper
¹/₄ teaspoon cayenne pepper
1 cup Fennel Sauce (See recipe, page 256)
Fresh parsley for garnish

1. Preheat oven to 350° F.

2. Purée fish in the container of a food processor or blender, a small amount at a time. Place puréed mixture in a bowl and set bowl on ice cubes in a larger bowl. Let stand until well chilled.

3. Add fish stock* gradually, then the egg whites and cream and mix to a smooth consistency. Add salt, pepper, and cayenne to taste.

4. Pour into a 3-quart mold, filling it only three-fourths full. Place the mold in a pan half-filled with hot water and bake for 15 minutes.

5. Heat Fennel Sauce in a separate pan, but do not boil.

6. When mousse is done, unmold onto a hot platter. Ladle sauce over mousse. Serve with a rice pilaf. Garnish with fresh parsley

* SEE GLOSSARY

SERVES: 6
PREPARATION TIME: 5 MINUTES, PLUS FENNEL SAUCE AND TIME FOR CHILLING
COOKING TIME: 15 MINUTES

CAFÉ CHAUVERON, MIAMI

The Forge's Rollades Norweigian

There is nothing that awakens the taste buds more than fresh dill. Serve extra sauce on the side for an elegant touch. Alvin Malnick, owner of the infamous Forge, would approve of this version.

12 strips of sole fillets, 1 1/2 inches wide
12 strips of Nova Scotia salmon, 1 1/2 inches wide
1 cup dry white wine
3/4 cup water
2 teaspoons fresh thyme, or 1 teaspoon dried
Dash salt, or to taste
Dash white pepper
1 onion, sliced
2 stalks celery, peeled and cut in large pieces
1 recipe Dill Sauce (see recipe, page 254)
Red lettuce leaves

1. Flatten strips of sole carefully with a flat mallet. Try to form strips of salmon the same size. Place salmon on sole strips. Roll up and secure roulades with a toothpick.

2. Bring wine, water, thyme, salt, pepper, onion, and celery to a boil. Reduce to a simmer. Place the roulades in the simmering broth. Cover the pan with foil and bake at 400° F. for 10 to 12 minutes or until fish flakes easily. Drain, cool, and then refrigerate.

3. To serve, trim ends to show red and white spirals. Place on lettuce leaves and cover with Dill Sauce.

SERVES: 12 AS A FIRST COURSE
PREPARATION TIME: 15 MINUTES, PLUS TIME FOR CHILLING
COOKING TIME: 10 TO 12 MINUTES

THE FORGE, MIAMI BEACH

Derby Lane's Salmon Canapés

Easy, delicious, and cool. This is a "no brainer" hors d'oeuvre to make and serve. Not exactly a dish for the dogs.

1 **8-ounce can salmon, chilled**
2 teaspoons grated onion
3 tablespoons light mayonnaise
1¹/₂ teaspoons lemon or lime juice
¹/₄ teaspoon Worcestershire sauce
¹/₂ teaspoon paprika
¹/₄ teaspoon salt
¹/₄ teaspoon Tabasco sauce
12 small rounds rye bread
12 thinly sliced dill pickle slices

1. Drain salmon. Flake into a small bowl. Add the grated onion, mayonnaise, lemon juice, Worcestershire sauce, paprika, salt, and Tabasco. Taste for seasoning.

2. Carefully spread salmon on rye bread rounds. Top with pickle slice.

MAKES: 12
PREPARATION TIME: 10 MINUTES

DERBY LANE RESTAURANT, ST. PETERSBURG

Café Chauveron's Salmon Parisienne

When in Paris (or Florida) do as the Parisians (and Floridians) do - eat well!
This classic dish looks more complicated than it is.

1 large, fresh salmon, 4 to 5 pounds, thickly sliced
1/2 cup red wine vinegar
1 onion, sliced
1 peeled carrot, sliced
2 stalks celery, peeled and halved
2 bay leaves, crushed
1 teaspoon thyme
1 tablespoon salt, or to taste
8 peppercorns
Fresh parsley
1 lemon or lime, sliced
Water

1. Place salmon in a fish poacher or large saucepan. Add the above ingredients, with the exception of the parsley and lemon, and cover with water. Slowly bring to a boiling point. If the fish is not cooked when the boiling point is reached, simmer until done. Watch carefully to make sure that you don't overcook.

2. Remove from the heat. Cool in the liquid. Carefully remove and take off skin and any bones. Place on a large platter and decorate with lemon slices and parsley.

3. Serve with homemade mayonnaise, tartar sauce, or Russian dressing. Other appropriate sauces would be sour cream with cucumber, herbed mayonnaise, or Café Chauveron's Fennel Sauce (see recipe, page 256). If a whole salmon is not available, salmon steaks can be used.

SERVES: 6
PREPARATION TIME: 5 MINUTES
COOKING TIME: 20 TO 25 MINUTES

CAFÉ CHAUVERON, MIAMI

King Charles' Smoked Salmon Stuffed With Crab Mousse

This restaurant has been replaced by one a lot less "prissy" than the old King Charles, but I still remember this elegant appetizer. Be sure to thoroughly cool this dish; it can be prepared ahead to conserve your energy for consumption.

STUFFING
¼ pound crab meat
¼ pound Nova Scotia smoked salmon
1 ounce heavy cream, or lighter
1 dash arrowroot
Dash fresh lime juice

1. Blend the crab and smoked salmon.

2. Dissolve the arrowroot in the heavy cream. Add the lime juice.

3. Mix the cream mixture into the crab and salmon.

MEDALLIONS
1 pound sliced smoked salmon

1. Lay salmon, side by side, on waxed paper. Place stuffing on the edge of the salmon closest to you and roll up. Refrigerate until firm, about 30 minutes.

2. Slice diagonally and serve with green sauce that follows.

PERFECT GREEN SAUCE
½ cup mayonnaise
2 tablespoons fresh parsley, finely chopped
2 tablespoons fresh watercress, finely chopped
2 tablespoons fresh spinach, finely chopped
1 tablespoon lemon or lime juice
¼ tablespoon Dijon mustard

1. Blend all ingredients. Refrigerate overnight before serving.

SERVES: 6 TO 8
PREPARATION TIME: 20 MINUTES PLUS TIME FOR CHILLING

KING CHARLES RESTAURANT AT THE DON CESAR HOTEL, ST. PETE BEACH

Amberjack With Creole Sauce

Ponce de Leon himself would have feasted on this delicious dish prepared in a quaint North Florida eatery. Amberjack is a member of the salmon family and every bit as good! Sauce is great on meat and eggs, too.

AMBERJACK FILLETS

6 6-ounce amberjack fillets
Lemon-butter (1/2 cup melted butter with 2 tablespoons lemon juice)
Paprika

1. Pat fillets flat with pounder, then broil in a melted lemon-butter sauce. Sprinkle paprika on top and set aside.

CREOLE SAUCE

1 onion, chopped
2 stalks celery, peeled and chopped
1 bell pepper, chopped
Bacon grease, or olive oil, about 1/4 cup
1 10-ounce can crushed tomatoes
1 4-ounce can tomato sauce
3 teaspoons prepared roux*
2 bay leaves, crushed
Pinch sweet basil
Dash hot sauce
Dash Worcestershire sauce
Dash soy sauce
Salt and cracked black pepper to taste

1. Prepare roux*. Prepare Creole Sauce. Sauté onion, celery, and bell pepper with a little bacon grease. Pour in tomatoes and tomato sauce. When mixture comes to a boil, add roux* to thicken. Add crushed bay leaves and boil; then add basil, hot sauce, Worcestershire sauce, soy sauce, salt, and pepper. Cook 10 minutes, or until mixture reaches gravy base consistency. Stir frequently.

2. Serve over fillets and a side of sauce on each dish.

* SEE GLOSSARY

SERVES: 6
PREPARATION TIME: 20 MINUTES
COOKING TIME: 20 MINUTES

COFFEE CUP, PENSACOLA

Marker 88's Yellowtail California

Yellowtail is abundant in the Florida Keys but not always easy to find elsewhere. This is an elegant preparation.

2 pounds yellowtail fillets, or other firm white fish
$1/4$ cup Worcestershire sauce and $1/4$ water
2 tablespoons lemon juice
Salt and white pepper to taste
All-purpose flour
1 egg beaten with $1/4$ cup milk
$1/4$ pound clarified butter* for sautéing
16 slices of tomato
2 small avocados, cut in $1/4$-inch slices
1 cup béarnaise sauce*
$1/2$ cup melted butter
$1/4$ cup additional lemon juice
Fresh parsley, chopped

1. Preheat oven to 450° F.

2. Season the fillets in a mixture of Worcestershire, lemon juice, salt, and white pepper. Dip in flour, then in beaten egg. Heat the clarified butter and sauté the fish on only one side.

3. Place in a 13" x 9" x 2" buttered baking dish and pour the pan juices over the fish. Top with a layer of tomato slices and then avocado. Bake 8 to 10 minutes. When done, remove from the heat and top with béarnaise sauce*.

4. Place under broiler until just browned. Top with mixture of melted butter, lemon juice, and parsley.

* SEE GLOSSARY

SERVES: 4
PREPARATION TIME: 10 MINUTES
COOKING TIME: 10 TO 15 MINUTES

MARKER 88, PLANTATION KEY

Marker 88's Yellowtail Port Of Spain

Try to catch yellowtail if you are in the Keys. It lends itself to many different preparations.

Follow directions for seasoning, sautéing, and baking in California Yellowtail Recipe (see page 45). Top with Port of Spain Sauce:

PORT OF SPAIN SAUCE

1 Recipe California Yellowtail (see page 45)
1/2 cup each diced bananas, apples, and pimientos
1/2 cup peeled, seeded, and diced tomatoes
Butter
Juice of 1 lemon
1 tablespoon chopped fresh parsley

1. Simmer all ingredients together until heated through. Pour on top of baked yellowtail.

SERVES: 4
PREPARATION TIME: 12 MINUTES
COOKING TIME: 10 TO 15 MINUTES

MARKER 88, PLANTATION KEY

Dominique's Simmered Fresh Tuna

Fresh swordfish or salmon can be used as a replacement for the tuna. The lettuce acts as a "moisturizer" and can be served wrapped around the fish or taken off and served on the side as a tasty garnish.

4 8-ounce tuna steaks, about 1¹/4 inches thick
Juice of 2 lemons
1 Spanish onion, thinly sliced
¹/4 cup extra virgin olive oil
¹/2 cup diced celery
8 large leaves of Boston lettuce, blanched* in water for 2 minutes
4 anchovy fillets, rinsed in cold water and chopped
2 tablespoons chopped fresh dill, or 1 tablespoon dried
Salt and cracked black pepper to taste
1¹/3 cups dry white wine
¹/2 cup chopped fresh parsley
4 lemon wedges

1. Place steaks in a deep non-metallic pan and cover with water. Add lemon juice water. Boil for 2 minutes and discard liquid.

2. Place onion, extra virgin olive oil, and celery into a large saucepan and place steaks on top of mixture. Slowly brown the fish steaks over a low heat. When brown, turn over and arrange the anchovies and dill on top and season with salt and cracked black pepper to taste.

3. When the fish is done (translucent), remove it from the pan and tightly wrap each steak in 2 lettuce leaves. Return to the pan, covered, and gradually add the butter and the wine. Simmer 20 to 25 minutes or until done.

4. Place the steaks in a 2-inch-deep serving platter and top with pan juices, vegetables, and chopped parsley. Serve lemon wedges on the side.

* SEE GLOSSARY

SERVES: 4
PREPARATION TIME: 20 MINUTES
COOKING TIME: 25 MINUTES

DOMINIQUE'S, MIAMI BEACH, WASHINGTON, D.C.

Fontainebleau's Sole in Savoy Cabbage

Prepare this dish early. Make stuffing and roll the cabbage leaves in the morning and keep refrigerated. Then, just before serving, simmer the cabbage rolls and make the Champagne Sauce. This dish will simply melt in your mouth!

SOLE STUFFING

5 pounds fresh sole, well chilled
2 tablespoons butter
1/2 cup white bread crumbs
1/2 teaspoon salt
1/4 teaspoon white pepper
Dash of garlic powder
Dash of tarragon
Dash of basil
1/4 cup champagne
3 ice cubes

1. To prepare cabbage stuffing, combine all ingredients in the container of a food processor or blender. Blend on very high speed. Do this quickly to avoid the stuffing becoming warm. Place mixture in refrigerator.

CABBAGE

1 head Savoy cabbage
2 cups dry white wine
1/2 cup water
2 cups fish bouillon, or 1 cup chicken bouillon and 1 cup water
1 Recipe Sole Stuffing

CONTINUED...

1. Remove 8 very large outer leaves from the cabbage. Place leaves in simmering mixture of dry white wine and water. Blanch until they are opaque and tender but firm. Remove leaves. Dry each leaf on paper towels, lying leaves flat. Reserve wine-water mixture.

2. Divide stuffing into 8 equal portions. Place each portion on 1 leaf of cabbage, wrapping cabbage around stuffing in rolled form. Place rolls in refrigerator and chill for 1 1/2 to 2 hours.

3. Add fish bouillon to wine-water mixture. Bring to boil, then reduce to simmer. Add the cabbage rolls and simmer 12 to 15 minutes. Remove rolls. Place in warm oven (225° F.) on serving platter. Prepare Champagne Sauce to follow.

CHAMPAGNE SAUCE

1 cup fish bouillon, strained from above
1/2 pint heavy cream
2 to 3 tablespoons butter
1/4 cup champagne or other sparkling white wine
2 ounces caviar

1. In a heavy saucepan, combine bouillon, heavy cream, and butter and bring to simmer. Add champagne and simmer for another minute.

2. Pour champagne sauce over the cabbage rolls and sprinkle with caviar.

SERVES: 4 ENTRÉES OR 8 APPETIZERS
PREPARATION TIME: 45 MINUTES
COOKING TIME: 30 MINUTES

THE DINING GALLERIES AT THE FONTAINEBLEAU HILTON, MIAMI BEACH

Brothers' Sole in Nut Sauce

It is sometimes difficult to get hazelnuts. If that is the case, substitute with half pine nuts, half almonds. If you don't have Melba toast on hand, toast a thin piece of bread and then let it dry out on a rack. You will go nuts over this wonderful dish from a long-gone, but much-remembered Tampa Bay restaurant.

4 center slices of sole
3 cups Fumé de Poisson (fish stock*)
10 blanched* almonds
15 hazelnuts (filberts)
2 tablespoons pine nuts (pignoli)
2 tablespoons chopped parsley
Pinch of saffron, optional
1 small clove garlic, crushed
1/2 slice Melba toast
Salt and white pepper
8 sprigs of dill

1. Preheat oven to 350° F.

2. Poach* the sole in boiling fish stock for 3 minutes. Watch closely to make sure that it does not overcook. Drain well, reserve stock, and place in an oven-proof serving dish.

3. Reserve 4 each of all the nuts for garnish. Grind the remainder with the Melba toast. Mix ground nuts into the parsley, garlic, and saffron.

4. Reduce* the reserved stock to 2 cups. Add nut mixture. Season to taste with salt and white pepper. Pour sauce over fish and bake until sauce is heated through. Garnish with dill and reserved nuts.

* SEE GLOSSARY

SERVES: 4
PREPARATION TIME: 10 MINUTES
COOKING TIME: 10 TO 15 MINUTES

BROTHERS, TOO, TAMPA

Marty's Sautéed Fillet of Sole

A Spanish specialty reminiscent of my last visit to the beautiful city of Madrid.

4 6-ounce fillets of sole
4 bananas, sliced crosswise
¹/₄ clarified butter*
1 cup hollandaise sauce*
Rice pilaf
Broccoli flowerets
Baby carrots

1. Preheat oven to 350° F.

2. Place sole fillet in a greased non-metallic square shallow baking pan and brush with clarified butter*. Arrange the banana slices over the pieces of sole. Bake until done (translucent), about 10 minutes, depending upon size of fish.

3. Place on attractive plate and spoon on hollandaise sauce*. Serve with rice pilaf, fresh broccoli flowerets, and baby carrots.

* SEE GLOSSARY

SERVES: 4 TO 6
PREPARATION TIME: 10 MINUTES
COOKING TIME: 10 MINUTES

MARTY'S STEAKS, TAMPA

Fontainebleau's Stuffed Pompano

You will never have such a delicious pompano sandwich. Chef Tevini, who has since moved on, created this incredibly delectable dish nearly 15 years ago, but that first forkful is still vividly remembered.

2 2¹/₂ pound pompano fillets
1 pint milk
¹/₂ cup butter
¹/₂ ounce chopped shallots
1 clove garlic, chopped
¹/₃ cup mushrooms, quartered
¹/₄ pound Alaskan king crab meat, picked through
¹/₂ pint heavy cream
¹/₂ teaspoon chopped fresh chives
Pinch each of basil, tarragon, salt, white pepper
Juice of 1 lemon
¹/₂ cup all-purpose flour
2 eggs, lightly beaten

1. Preheat oven to 350° F.

2. Soak fillets in milk for a few minutes to remove any fishy taste.

3. Melt ¹/₄ cup of butter and add shallots, garlic, and mushrooms and sauté for 30 seconds. Stir in crab meat and cook until just heated through. Add heavy cream and chives. Simmer until thick. Season with basil, tarragon, salt, pepper, and lemon juice. Remove from heat and let cool.

4. Using clean hands, sandwich mixture between 2 fillets. Dip pieces carefully into flour, shake off excess, and then dip in egg. Melt the remaining butter and sauté the fish until brown on both sides.

5. Place in preheated oven for 10 to 15 minutes.

SERVES: 2
PREPARATION TIME: 10 MINUTES
COOKING TIME: 20 TO 25 MINUTES

THE DINING GALLERIES AT THE FONTAINEBLEAU HILTON, MIAMI BEACH

Bay Harbor Island Pompano Veronique

You can prepare this dish with any fresh firm white fish. Serve with spinach or broccoli and rice to help sop up this "awesome" rich sauce.

4 pompano fillets, 1¼ pounds each (sole or any other white fish is a good substitute)
1 teaspoon salt
Cracked black pepper to taste
4 tablespoons butter or extra virgin olive oil
4 shallots, chopped
3 cups dry white wine such as Chardonnay
½ cup cream sauce
4 tablespoons heavy cream, whipped
1 cup Muscat grapes, seeded and skinned

1. Preheat broiler.

2. Season fish fillets with salt and cracked black pepper to taste and place in a large, heavy saucepan or fish poacher. Dot with 2 tablespoons butter or extra virgin olive oil and sprinkle with shallots. Add wine. Bring to a boil and simmer slowly for 20 to 30 minutes or until fish are just done. Remove fish to an oven-proof serving dish.

3. Reduce* liquid in saucepan until it is reduced to a third of its original quantity.

4. Work 2 tablespoons of butter or extra virgin olive oil into the cream sauce, then stir into liquid. Correct seasoning and stir in the whipped cream.

5. Place grapes around the fish and pour the sauce over all. Brown under a hot broiler.

* SEE GLOSSARY

SERVES: 4
PREPARATION TIME: 10 MINUTES
COOKING TIME: 30 MINUTES

CAFÉ CHAUVERON, MIAMI

St. Petersburg Mullet à la Paysanne

Rollande et Pierre Restaurant has been replaced by The Melting Pot, but I can still remember the great flavors my guests and I enjoyed—nearly twenty years ago!! In place of the mullet you may use other fish such as redfish, red snapper, or grouper. A good, hearty, country-style way to prepare your favorite fish.

3 medium-size mullet, whole, or equivalent amount of fillets
1 lemon, sliced
2 tablespoons butter or extra virgin olive oil
4 medium ripe tomatoes, diced
2 medium green bell peppers, diced
1/2 cup sliced onions
1/3 cup extra virgin olive oil
1 clove garlic, crushed
1 bay leaf
Pinch of thyme
Salt and cracked black pepper to taste
1/2 cup dry white wine or dry vermouth
1/4 cup chopped fresh parsley for garnish

1. Preheat oven to 350° F.

2. Clean the mullet and pat dry or have the fishmonger do it for you. Place them in a buttered 13" x 9" x 2" baking dish. Place 2 slices of lemon on top of each fillet and dot with butter or extra virgin olive oil.

3. In a heavy skillet cook tomatoes, green bell peppers, and onions in extra virgin olive oil. Add crushed garlic, bay leaf, and thyme. Stir and cook for 5 minutes. Season to taste with salt and cracked black pepper.

4. Place the vegetable mixture around the fish. Pour the wine or vermouth over the fish and the vegetables. Bake for about 20 to 30 minutes, 15 minutes if you use fillets. Garnish with the chopped parsley and serve immediately.

SERVES: 3
PREPARATION TIME: 15 MINUTES
COOKING TIME: 20 TO 35 MINUTES

ROLLANDE ET PIERRE, ST. PETERSBURG

Buttonwood's Smoked Mullet

There's another bar-restaurant where Buttonwood once operated, yet I'll never forget the luscious taste of Buttonwood's fresh mullet!

4 fresh whole mullet
Salt and cracked black pepper to taste
Garlic salt to taste
1 tablespoon Hungarian paprika

1. Remove full fillet from each side of fish. Leave skin and scales on to act as a retainer for juices. Soak fillets approximately 2 hours in salted water. Remove and place on grill in smoker. Season with salt, pepper, garlic, and paprika.

2. Smoke with buttonwood mangrove**, if available. Smoke according to directions until flaky, about 3 to 4 hours, at 195° F.

** A SPECIAL WOOD FROM THE FLORIDA MANGROVES, BUT ANY NICELY, LIGHT-FLAVORED WOOD CHIPS WILL DO.

SERVES: 4
PREPARATION TIME: 2 HOURS TO SOAK
COOKING TIME: 3 TO 4 HOURS

BUTTONWOOD BAR-B-Q, SANIBEL ISLAND

Buttonwood's Smoked Mullet Spread

Wonderful on crackers or as a spread for a sandwich!

2 to 3 fillets smoked mullet
$1/2$ cup chopped onion
$1/2$ cup chopped green bell pepper
$1/4$ cup chopped celery
1 8-ounce package cream cheese
$1/4$ to $1/2$ cup mayonnaise
Horseradish to taste
Paprika

1. Peel fish from skin and break into small pieces. Remove all bones and cartilage. Set aside.

2. Add onion, green bell pepper, and celery to cream cheese and mix together to a smooth consistency. Add prepared smoked mullet. Form into a ball and sprinkle with paprika. Refrigerate.

SERVES: 6 AS AN HORS D'OEUVRE
PREPARATION TIME: 10 MINUTES
ALLOW TIME FOR CHILLING

BUTTONWOOD BAR-B-Q, SANIBEL ISLAND

Gary's Flounder en Papillote

Serve the aromatic fillets on an attractive platter and don't cut open until the plates are set before the lucky recipients. The aroma will excite!

4 6-ounce flounder fillets
1/4 pound plus 2 tablespoons butter
1 cup all-purpose flour
1 quart milk
1 cup finely chopped scallions
1 cup sliced mushrooms, fresh or canned
1/2 teaspoon salt
1 teaspoon Worcestershire sauce
1/2 teaspoon Tabasco sauce
Dash of white pepper
Juice of one lemon
3/4 cup sherry
Parchment paper
Vegetable oil
12 large cooked shrimp

1. Preheat oven to 400° F.

2. In a large frying pan, melt the 1/4 pound butter and stir in flour to make a roux*. Cook, stirring about 3 minutes. Gradually add milk and stir until thick.

3. Melt remaining 2 tablespoons of butter, then sauté scallions and mushrooms for 5 minutes. Stir entire contents of pan into cream sauce along with the seasonings and lemon juice. Set aside to cool.

4. Steam flounder in sherry for 2 minutes. Turn carefully.

5. Cut parchment paper into 12-inch square pieces, 1 per fillet. Grease both sides of paper with vegetable oil. Place 2 tablespoons or more of sauce in the middle of each paper and place a fillet on top. Top each fillet with 3 shrimp and 3 more tablespoons or more of cream sauce. Fold paper over and twist ends. Bake 10 minutes. Cut open while hot. Remove parchment if you desire.

*SEE GLOSSARY

SERVES: 4
PREPARATION TIME: 15 MINUTES
COOKING TIME: 15 TO 20 MINUTES

GARY'S DUCK INN, ORLANDO

Dominique's Fresh Swordfish Grillé

The marinade helps keep the swordfish juicy. Shark or other slightly oily fin fish are other good substitutes.

4 8- to 14-ounce swordfish steaks, about 1 inch thick
Juice of 3 lemons
1½ cups extra virgin olive oil
½ cup dry white wine
2 cloves garlic, crushed
3 tablespoons finely chopped fresh parsley
½ teaspoon fresh oregano
Salt and freshly ground black pepper
Lemon wedges

1. Preheat broiler.

2. Mix lemon juice, extra virgin olive oil, wine, garlic, parsley, oregano, salt, and pepper in a non-metallic bowl. Marinate swordfish in mixture for about 1 hour or more. Drain and reserve marinade.

3. Broil fish, turning once, basting with the marinade occasionally. When fish is golden brown, cut into 2" cubes. Season with parsley, salt, and cracked black pepper to taste to taste. Mix in remaining marinade.

4. Bake in 400° F. oven for about 5 minutes. Serve with lemon wedges.

SERVES: 4
PREPARATION TIME: 10 MINUTES, PLUS TIME TO MARINATE
COOKING TIME: APPROXIMATELY 15 MINUTES

DOMINIQUE'S, MIAMI BEACH, WASHINGTON, D.C

Shad Roe Dominique

For those not familiar with these choice fish eggs, shad roe must be experienced. The roe should have a clean aroma and should be firm and moist. Fresh roe is available in the spring.

2 pairs fresh shad roe
Salt and freshly ground black pepper
1/3 cup all-purpose flour
2/3 cups unsalted butter or extra virgin olive oil
2 tablespoons Worcestershire sauce
Juice of 1 lemon
4 tablespoons chopped fresh chives
2 tablespoons chopped fresh parsley
8 crisp bacon slices, optional

1. Carefully cut off the skin connecting the pairs of roe. Sprinkle roe with salt and cracked black pepper to taste and dip into flour, shaking off excess.

2. In a large heavy skillet melt 6 tablespoons of the butter or extra virgin olive oil over medium-high heat until it sizzles. Add roe and cook them about 5 minutes on each side or until golden brown. Remove roe to a warm serving platter.

3. Add all remaining ingredients, except bacon, to the pan juices. Bring to a quick boil.

4. Pour over the roe. Serve roe with the crisp cooked bacon.

SERVES: 4
PREPARATION TIME: 5 MINUTES
COOKING TIME: 15 MINUTES

DOMINIQUE'S, MIAMI BEACH, WASHINGTON, D.C.

Cruise Inn's Stuffed Perch Oscar

This dish alone is an entire meal. Purchase the crab cake as crab stuffing at the fish market, to save time. Better yet, when you make your own crab cakes (see recipe, page 135), freeze some for this recipe. Borrowed from the folks at the old Cruise Inn (who really know about seafood), this is a blue-ribbon winner!

6 ounces medium size shrimp
1/2 pound asparagus spears
1 1/2 pounds thin fillets of perch
1/2 to 3/4 pounds crab cake
1 1/2 cups hollandaise sauce*
Seasoned salt
Salt and pepper to taste
Fresh parsley for garnish

1. Clean, shell, and devein the shrimp. Refrigerate.

2. Trim, peel, and wash the asparagus. Cook until almost done. While the asparagus is boiling, line a 13" x 9" x 2" shallow baking dish with half of the fillets. Spread a layer of crab cake over them. Arrange the rest of the fillets on top. Bake for 15 minutes at 425° F.

3. While perch is cooking, prepare the hollandaise sauce*. Keep warm atop a double broiler to prevent from burning.

4. Remove the perch from the oven. Lay the asparagus spears across the top and place the shrimp between and at each end of the asparagus. Cover with the hollandaise sauce and sprinkle with seasoned salt. Salt and pepper to taste.

5. Return dish to the oven and bake for another 10 minutes.

6. When ready to serve, add fresh parsley for garnish.

* SEE GLOSSARY

SERVES: 4 TO 6
PREPARATION TIME: 30 MINUTES
COOKING TIME: 30 MINUTES

CRUISE INN, PALMETTO

Ted Peters' Smoked Fish Spread

Ted Peters is my favorite place for smoked mullet and mackerel. It's been that way for 31 years — since the first time I bit into my first taste of the fresh smoked fish. There is nothing quite as delicious. Ted's smokes this "spread" from their quality fish. It's so good, you could eat a whole gallon yourself.

3¹/₂ quarts flaked smoked fish, de-boned, mullet preferred
2 cups finely diced onion
1 cup finely diced celery
1¹/₂ cups sweet relish with pimiento
1¹/₄ quarts white salad dressing

1. Mix together fish, onion, celery, relish, and salad dressing. Chill. Best if served in 2 to 3 days.

SERVES: A PARTY
PREPARATION TIME: 10 MINUTES

TED PETERS FAMOUS SMOKED FISH, ST. PETERSBURG

Mahi-Mahi Lazarra

Co-owner Steve Knight improvised this dish on the spur of the moment and named it after his partner, Bob Lazzara. Try this inspiration!

1 pineapple, skinned and cored, reserve the leaves
4 medium green bell peppers, sliced
1 medium red onion, sliced
1 tablespoon butter or extra virgin olive oil
1 teaspoon garlic salt**
2 cloves garlic, minced
1¹/₂ cups crushed or stewed tomatoes
3¹/₂ pounds mahi-mahi, substitute shark or swordfish if mahi-mahi not available
¹/₂ teaspoon salt
¹/₂ teaspoon garlic powder
2 tablespoons butter at room temperature

CONTINUED...

1. Quarter and then slice pineapple on a wooden board. Remove pineapple but reserve any juices that remain on the board. Slice (medium) the peppers and onion on the same board so that they will soak up some of the flavor of the remaining juices.

2. Melt butter and sprinkle with garlic salt. Sauté the peppers and garlic in the butter until the garlic is brown but not burned. Remove with a slotted spoon. Brown onions in same pan and then return the peppers, garlic, and half of the pineapple to the pan. Try to squeeze some juice onto the vegetables.

3. Mix 1/2 teaspoon salt, garlic powder, and softened butter together and rub into fish. Place fish in pan over pepper mixture. Cook over a medium heat until fish has become translucent.

4. Turn the fish over and reduce heat to low. Cook about 7 minutes.

5. Fold pepper mixture over fish and add the tomatoes, which have been heated. Simmer for about 15 minutes.

6. Serve on a tray decorated with the remaining half of the pineapple and the reserved pineapple leaves.

** FRESH GARLIC IS HIGHLY RECOMMENDED, BUT THE RESTAURANT USED SALT

SERVES: 7
PREPARATION TIME: 20 MINUTES
COOKING TIME: APPROXIMATELY 30 TO 40 MINUTES

CAP'S SEAFOOD RESTAURANT, ST. AUGUSTINE

Black Sea Bass St. Augustine

Klaus is perhaps one of Florida's best chefs. His restaurant has been gone for years, but this recipe is a fine example of his excellent gastronomic skills. You can substitute other firm fish, but I shall always remember Klaus' awesome bass. Begin by preparing the stuffing first.

SEA BASS STUFFING
   2 tablespoons chopped shallots
   2 tablespoons chopped scallions
   1/4 cup butter or extra virgin olive oil
   4 ounces all-purpose flour
   1/2 cup light cream
   1/2 pound king crab meat, chopped and picked through
   1 ounce white wine, such as Chardonnay
   Salt to taste
   Pepper to taste
   1 teaspoon lemon juice or lime juice
   1 cup bread crumbs
   2 medium eggs, whipped lightly with a fork

1. Sauté the shallots and scallions in the butter until tender. Whisk in the flour and stir constantly to make a roux*. Simmer 5 to 10 minutes. Add the cream and heat just to boiling. Lower heat and simmer, stirring to make smooth.

2. Add the crab meat, wine, salt, pepper, and lemon or lime juice. Taste and adjust the seasonings. Remove from heat. Add the bread crumbs and the eggs, and mix well. The filling should be stiff but spreadable. Chill.

* SEE GLOSSARY

CONTINUED...

FRESH BASS

4 12- to 16-ounce sea bass fillets
¼ cup lemon juice or lime juice
1 cup all-purpose flour
2 eggs, lightly beaten
Clarified butter* as needed
Hollandaise sauce*
Fresh parsley for garnish

1. Preheat oven to 350° F.

2. Flatten the bass, pour on the juice and marinate for about 15 minutes.

3. Spread the fillets with the prepared filling and roll up. Tie if necessary. Dredge each rolled fillet in flour and dip in the lightly beaten eggs.

4. Sauté the fillets in the butter until golden.

5. Bake for 20 to 25 minutes. Allow to rest 10 to 15 minutes before serving. Pour the hollandaise sauce* over the fillets. Garnish with fresh parsley.

* SEE GLOSSARY

SERVES: 6
PREPARATION TIME: 40 MINUTES
COOKING TIME: 40 MINUTES

KLAUS' CUISINE, DAYTONA BEACH

Half Shell's Smoked Fish Dip

Serve with crackers. You'll want to move to the Keys right now.

1 pound smoked kingfish, marlin, tuna, or other slightly oily fish
1 stalk of celery, peeled and trimmed
1/4 onion
Tabasco sauce to taste
Mayonnaise, about 1/4 to 1/2 cup, depending on preference
Fresh lime juice, about 1 to 2 tablespoons, or to taste
Crackers

1. Grind the smoked fish, celery, and onion into a mixing bowl using the paddle of the mixer. Blend at a slow speed.

2. Add enough mayonnaise to bind. Season with Tabasco and lime juice.

3. Serve with plenty of crackers.

SERVES: 6 TO 10 AS AN HORS D'OEUVRE
PREPARATION TIME: 5 MINUTES

HALF SHELL RAW BAR AT LAND'S END VILLAGE, KEY WEST

BOSS BASS

Freshwater Fin Fish

Florida is a freshwater fishing paradise. More than 200 species of fish can be found in its millions of acres of lakes and 12,000 miles of streams and rivers. Before you grab a line and pole, however, you'll probably need a license. They're usually available at your local bait and tackle shop, along with information about fishing restrictions and limits. Make sure you know which fish are "in season." People have been known to be arrested and/or fined for illegal catches.

Clean Your Catch

Cleaning your catch may not be as messy as you think. First, spread plenty of newspapers over your work area and have a bag handy for the entrails, bones and other unwanted fish parts. Wash any slime or dirt off the fish. With a sharp knife, carefully cut off both pectoral fins (the smaller fins attached to either side of the body). Then you'll need to see if the fish need scaling (not all do). Run the blade of a blunt knife from the tail to the head. If the scales come up easily, you'll need to take them off until the fish is smooth. Make sure you get all of them; the scales get stuck between your teeth!

Now it's time for those pesky bones. Freshwater fish have lighter bones than their saltwater relatives, and have been a source of frustration to many fish lovers. Cut along both sides of the dorsal fin (the one on top) for the length of the fish. With a quick pull, you should be able to pull off the fin and the connecting bone from tail to head. Then you can cut the head off right below the gills and the tail off where it joins the body.

To remove the gills, cut through the belly all the way to the gills. Make sure you get all parts of the gills. Scoop out the fish guts and reddish-brown kidney line.

Live and raw seafood may carry illness-causing bacteria. These are not a problem if you cook the fish **thoroughly**. The Saltwater Section of this cookbook (see page 11) has information on cooking fish, along with guidelines for choosing, freezing and thawing all fin fish.

Fat Content for a Selection of Freshwater Fish

Fat (6% to 20% or more)
Chub
Pike (Northern, Blue)
Smelt
Yellow Perch

Intermediate (2% to 6%)
Alewife
Bass (small and large)
Brook Trout
Buffalo Fish
Carp
Catfish
Drum (freshwater)
Pickerel
Sucker

Lean (Less than 2%)
Bullhead (black)
Crappie
Lake Trout
Mullet (striped)
Perch
Rainbow Trout
Salmon
Shad
Whitefish (lake)

Steve's St. Cloud Catfish

Here's how Steve and real Florida Crackers prepare this delectable meal. Use Old Bay® Seasoning instead of paprika if you prefer.

4 6- to 8-ounce catfish fillets, cut in 2- to 3-inch strips
1 cup stone ground cornmeal**
Salt and pepper to taste
Dash Hungarian paprika
Vegetable oil for frying

1. Lightly season cornmeal with salt and cracked black pepper to taste. Add a little paprika for color.

2. Dip catfish strips in meal mixture and deep fry until golden brown. Fish should be cooked evenly throughout.

** SIFT THE USED CORNMEAL TO GET RID OF LUMPS FROM THE DAMPNESS OF THE FISH EACH TIME YOU MAKE THIS RECIPE. STORE MEAL IN REFRIGERATOR AND RE-USE.

SERVES: 2 TO 4
PREPARATION TIME: 10 MINUTES
COOKING TIME: 5 TO 10 MINUTES

THE CATFISH PLACE, ST. CLOUD

Peter's Boneless Stuffed Trout

Peter sold a lot of these trout in his heyday. After he closed the restaurant, he became a full-time lawyer, gastronome, and travel aficionado.

If fresh "titi" shrimp are not available, use canned shrimp or small shrimp sliced and cut in small pieces. If you are going to grill the trout, lightly brush the grill with olive oil to prevent sticking. Finely chopped scallions can be used as a substitute for chives in a pinch.

2 large boneless brook or rainbow trout, trimmed and scaled
1/2 stick butter
1/2 cup sliced mushrooms
1/2 cup "titi" shrimp, well rinsed
2 teaspoons chopped chives
1/2 cup chopped sweet Vidalia onion, or other sweet onion
Dash white pepper and salt
1 teaspoon chopped green bell pepper
1 teaspoon anisette or Pernod
1 tablespoon fresh chopped parsley
Juice of 1/2 lemon
Toothpicks for trussing
Extra virgin olive oil

1. Melt 1/4 stick butter and sauté mushrooms until browned and soft. Melt other 1/4 stick of butter and sauté the shrimp, chives, and onion until onions are golden. Add anisette, parsley, pepper, and salt.

2. Stuff the trout with the hot mixture. Sprinkle with lemon juice and truss the trout with toothpicks. Using your hands, rub extra virgin olive oil all over the trout.

3. The trout can be cooked the following ways immediately after stuffing: on an open grill, broiled, or sautéed. In any case, figure 3 minutes per side or just until the flesh becomes white. Remove toothpicks. Serve on attractive plate with fresh vegetables.

SERVES: 2
PREPARATION TIME: 15 MINUTES
COOKING TIME: 6 MINUTES

PETER'S PLACE, ST. PETERSBURG

June Swanson's Troute Meuniere

The restaurant has been closed for ages, but this recipe continues in the hearts and minds of many Florida seafood lovers. Yum!

4 small freshwater trout, cleaned and boned
Garlic salt to taste
Salt and cracked black pepper to taste
1 cup all-purpose flour
4 tablespoons melted butter or extra virgin olive oil
4 teaspoons finely chopped shallots
4 teaspoons lemon juice
1/4 cup dry white sherry
Parsley
Lemon slices
Watercress

1. Sprinkle trout with garlic salt about 1 hour before cooking.

2. Season with salt and cracked black pepper to taste. Dip in flour and shake off excess. Melt butter or use olive oil until sizzling. Cook trout until both sides are brown and the flesh is cooked. Transfer to a large platter.

3. Add a little more butter or olive oil to the same pan. Sauté the shallots until translucent and add lemon juice and sherry. Deglaze* pan and pour remaining juices over trout. Garnish with parsley, lemon, and watercress.

* SEE GLOSSARY

SERVES: 4
PREPARATION TIME: 5 MINUTES
COOKING TIME: ABOUT 10 MINUTES

SWANSON'S BISTRO AND WINE BAR, CLEARWATER

Rollande's Trout Braised in Champagne

Another classic from St. Petersburg's colorful (and flavorful) past.

1/4 **pound butter or extra virgin olive oil**
1 **shallot, chopped**
1 **onion, chopped**
2 **carrots, cut in julienne** *
2 **celery stalks, trimmed and cut in julienne**
1 **2-pound fresh trout or 4 10-ounce trout, boned**
4 **slices bacon**
1 **head of lettuce, leaves separated**
Salt and pepper
2 **cups champagne or sparkling wine**
2 **tablespoons heavy cream, or may use lighter cream**

1. Preheat oven to 400° F.

2. Melt butter or add olive oil to pan. Simmer shallot, onion, carrots, and celery for 5 minutes. Remove vegetables with a slotted spoon and reserve the melted butter or oil.

3. Stuff the trout with the vegetables. Wrap bacon slices around the trout and then wrap in the lettuce leaves.

4. Place trout into a 11" x 7" x 2" oven-proof baking dish and brush with the reserved butter or oil. Sprinkle with salt and cracked black pepper to taste and pour champagne over all. Bake for 20 minutes. Remove from oven and remove the bacon and lettuce.

5. Add the cream and return to the oven for about 2 minutes or until the cream has heated through.

* SEE GLOSSARY

SERVES: 4
PREPARATION TIME: 15 MINUTES
COOKING TIME: 25 MINUTES

ROLLANDE ET PIERRE, ST. PETERSBURG

Casa Vecchia Trout Primavera

Leonce Picot, one of Florida's earliest gastronomes, gave me the recipe for this delightful dish. This restaurant is no longer operating, but one must never forget this glorious recipe!

¹/₄ pound butter
2 carrots, cut in julienne*
1 zucchini cut in julienne
Handful of snow pea pods, cut in julienne
1 green bell pepper, cut in julienne
1 small onion, peeled and cut in julienne
1 can pimientos, cut in julienne
2 celery stalks, trimmed and cut in julienne
2 tablespoons fresh basil
Salt and cracked black pepper to taste
2 fresh trout fillets, 12 to 14 ounces each
1 cup milk for dipping
1 cup all-purpose flour
2 cups hollandaise sauce*
1 cup whipping cream

1. Melt butter in large, heavy skillet. Add carrots, zucchini, snow pea pods, green pepper, onion, pimientos and celery. Sauté until cooked but still crunchy, about 5 minutes. Season with basil, salt, and cracked black pepper to taste. Set aside.

2. Dip fish fillets in milk. Dust with flour and sauté on both sides. Place in large baking dish. Top with vegetable mixture.

3. Mix hollandaise* with whipping cream. Keep warm.

4. Heat trout and vegetables in 325° F. oven. Serve with hollandaise-cream mixture over top.

* SEE GLOSSARY

SERVES: 2 TO 3
PREPARATION TIME: 15 MINUTES
COOKING TIME: 15 MINUTES

CASA VECCHIA, FORT LAUDERDALE

BOILED SHRIMP

Shrimp

Hooked

Americans eat about 800 million pounds of shrimp annually. It's our favorite shellfish, it's available in these parts year-round, and it's actually good for us. At a cost of about 30 calories per ounce, shrimp is a great source for protein and vitamin B and offers a bit of iron on the side, though it is higher in cholesterol than most fin fish. Shrimp has very little fat, and it's mostly those good-for-you omega-3 fatty acids, which help prevent strokes and heart attacks. It's one of the most versatile delicacies available!

Of course, this is assuming you are planning to steam the shrimp or cook it another low-fat way. Frying shrimp nullifies any good deed you may have done by buying it.

From Sea to Shining Sea

Most of the shrimp we choose at local markets come from our own back yard: the Gulf of Mexico, which is by far the largest shrimp fishery in the United States. More than 200 million pounds of our shrimp are caught there, more than double that caught anywhere else along the nation. Of course, that number pales in comparison to the nearly 600 million shrimp the United States imports from 40 or so different countries. The biggest foreign exporters are Thailand, Ecuador, Mexico, India, and China.

Most imported shrimp probably were farm-raised, while nearly all of the catch in the United States is wild.

One Shrimp, Two Shrimp, Three Shrimp, Four

Of the hundreds of shrimp species worldwide, you probably will only run across a few at your local Florida market. Though it may be tough to distinguish between them, the different types do have distinct colors and sometimes-subtle differences in taste. Here is where the fun begins.

Gulf White shrimp, which are actually grayish white with a green, blue, or red tinge on the tail, are often the most expensive and the best tasting because of their delectable flavor.

Gulf Pink, also high quality, are usually more red but vary in color based on where they are harvested. Along the Atlantic coast, they are more of a brown; along the northern Gulf coast, a lemony yellow; and in the Florida Tortugas, a pink.

Gulf Royal Red shrimp are usually a deep red color but also have a tendency to be grayish pink.

Gulf Brown, a reddish brown, are considered the least desirable because they are the most likely to taste like iodine, a natural mineral, especially the large ones.

Rock shrimp, which look a lot like small lobster tails, are deep-water shrimp caught off the mid-Atlantic and Southern states and in the Gulf of Mexico. They have a respectable flavor hidden under their Hulk Hogan-like shell. In fact, for a long time they were not readily available in the shell. They usually were sold already peeled and cooked because they are so difficult to peel. Today, though, you will find them frozen or fresh, whole or headless, with shell or without. Many of our seafood restaurants serve them with a lemony-garlic sauce.

Black Tiger shrimp, farmed from Asia, are the only type of shrimp that are a bit more colorful. They typically will be dark gray with black stripes and have red feelers or will be bluish with yellow feelers. They usually are very delicious and firm and often lower in price.

One Size Doesn't Fit All

Chances are, your recipe may not specifically call for one of these types of shrimp, but a good recipe will indicate the size of shrimp to purchase. Be aware what size will best suit your recipe. Shrimp can vary from bite-size pieces to bodies a few inches long. Though a variety of shrimp sizes are interchangeable, some work better than others do in certain recipes. Salads, for instance, seem like a natural for small shrimp, while grilling calls for shrimp that are larger and not likely to fall through the grill.

Colossal shrimp, many seafood lovers (myself included) will agree, are the best choice. The norm is ten or fewer to the pound. From there, sizes step down to extra large or jumbo, large, medium, and small, which can yield as many as seventy or so shrimp to the pound. The counts and classifications depend on your market.

Many chefs and "seafoodies" believe the best compromise in size is shrimp from fifteen or twenty to the pound. These shrimp offer great flavor, are easier to clean than small shrimp, and are less expensive than the high-priced colossal shrimp. Remember that labor spent fixing the critters should count!

It's your choice. All sizes of shrimp will give you basically the same flavor and food value. Just remember that shrimp shrink when cooked and shelled. A good rule of thumb is that two pounds of raw, headless, un-peeled shrimp net about one pound cooked and peeled.

What to Look for

Like fish, most shrimp were flash-frozen after being scooped up from the sea. Then once at your seafood market, they were either kept that way or thawed just before put on display—which can be referred to as previously frozen.

For that reason, some chefs like to buy raw shrimp still frozen. You can control the thawing yourself and cook at your convenience, but still retain the freshness and flavor that might have been lost by a less-than-careful store. Frozen raw shrimp can be less expensive, too.

If you choose to go that route, just make sure the shrimp—which should have shells but may or may not have the heads—are frozen solid with no brown spots or signs of freezer burn and have a white, dry appearance around the edges. Also, there should be little or no odor, though this might be hard to determine when well packed.

If your market offers it, opt for raw shrimp individually frozen instead of those clumped together in blocks. This way, you can thaw and cook a few at a time, rather than the whole bunch. Shrimp freeze well; flavors are retained better than nearly any other seafood.

The Color of Shrimp

When buying raw shrimp fresh, or "green" as some markets call it, look for shiny, moist, translucent, uncrushed meat—in shells—which has no ammonia or iodine odor. The bodies should be firm with little discoloration, which can come in the form of yellowing or brown spots. (Keep in mind black tiger shrimp have black rings.) Brown spots indicate the meat is starting to turn; yellowing or a gritty feel sometimes comes from trying to bleach brown spots. (Yes! There are those who do this!) Though the color of raw shrimp can vary from a transparent light brown to gray to pink, watch out for white meat, which shows freezer burn. Shells should fit tightly around the meat of the shrimp. Shrinkage is a sure sign of staleness.

Shrimp with heads deteriorate more quickly than those sold without the heads, which is probably the reason most stores sell shrimp headless. And most Americans don't relish the idea of those beady little eyes staring up at them. True culinarians (such as yourselves), however, will appreciate the beauty head-on shrimp afford a plate presentation. If you do buy head-on shrimp, make sure the heads are attached firmly to the bodies.

When choosing raw shrimp, pass by any that are pre-peeled or deveined. Cleaning them before freezing probably will deprive you of flavor and texture. Cooked shrimp are another story. They can be bought with or without the shell, intact. Either way, the meat should be firm to the touch, still look moist, and have turned a pearly white with pink and red shading. Cooked shells should be pink to red. Lastly, canned shrimp can be used for some of these recipes, but are not recommended. As with most great cuisine, fresh is best.

Now and Laters

When you get home, quickly refrigerate your catch or purchase at 32° to 38° F. then quickly freeze. Fresh or previously frozen raw shrimp—except for rock shrimp, which are highly perishable—will keep a day or two; cooked shrimp, up to three days.

Never re-freeze previously frozen raw shrimp or cooked shrimp. However, a package you bought already frozen can be put back in the freezer for about six months, provided the shrimp are well-wrapped and protected in airtight containers. If you have any doubts about leaving shrimp that long, it never hurts to err on the conservative side and toss them.

To freeze fresh raw shrimp, rinse the shrimp well, wrap in plastic freezer wrap or freezer bags, then seal in small bags so you can pull out just the amount you need when you decide to cook them. If you know it will be quite a while before you will use them, remove the heads for quality's sake.

Thaw frozen shrimp the same way you would thaw frozen fish: over a long period of time in the refrigerator or under cold, running water, without water and shrimp touching directly.

Knowing When to Stop

Shrimp can be prepared in any number of ways. They're perfect for everything from grilled kabobs and stuffed dishes to soups and salads. And they've been on the menu since the time of Confucius, who had words of praise for them even then.

There is only one rule to follow when cooking shrimp, and it applies to all shapes, colors, and sizes. Never overcook shrimp. Shrimp can cook in as little as two to four minutes—rock shrimp even quicker—so realize that when they're pink, they're done.

Cooked shrimp should have a white interior, a firm shape and feel, a succulent look, and a sweet smell.

Many chefs recommend keeping the shell on through cooking because you will end up with a better flavor. But if you must, remove the shells and save them. You can grind the shells in a food processor to make a shrimp butter or complete a sauce.

Removing the Robe

There are many ways you can de-robe your shrimp once they've cooked, or, in some cases, before.

My favorite method is to use a heavy steel shrimp deveiner which both deveins and removes the shell (see package directions). Plastic deveiners will do, but they tend to break. If you're a hands-on cook, hold the tail of the cooked shrimp in one hand while you slip the thumb of the other hand under the shell and between the feelers at the large end of the shrimp. Then, lift off two or three segments of the shell and gently ease the shrimp out. There should be no legs remaining, but if you prefer, you can leave the last section and the tail intact.

If you'd rather use scissors, try this method: Hold each shrimp with the head toward you and insert the scissors under the shell on the top (back) of the shrimp. Cut the shell down to the next to last section before the tail. The shell should just peel off.

Or, just start ripping away. One way or another, the shell needs to come off.

Any method you choose will leave the vein exposed. Removing this black threadlike digestive tract is purely for appearance's sake. Though it is not all that appealing to look it, the vein will not alter the taste of the shrimp if left in place. But (not surprisingly!) most people prefer to eat shrimp without the vein. Make a shallow cut lengthwise along the back of the shrimp and, holding the shrimp under running water, remove the vein with your fingers, a knife tip, or a toothpick. Don't forget to rinse (the shrimp and you) when you're done.

Shrimp Chests

For the "frugal gourmet," one of my most unusual methods of cooking the "chest" of the shrimps (the area just below the shrimp head that is usually chopped off), is one I learned at El Toccorro Restaurant in Havana, Cuba. Tomas, the famous Cuban chef would save the "chests", marinate them in a mojo (Spanish marinade of oil, garlic, and lime) then deep-fry them in extra virgin olive oil and lard. They were served as the house appetizer in his restaurant. As you might guess they were deliciously crunchy!!

Bob's Shrimp Rockefeller

The original owner, Bob Heilman, gave this delectable recipe to me. His son, Bob Jr., continues the favorite family traditions. The shrimp and spinach base can be made earlier in the day and refrigerated. A richly Rockefeller dish!

BOILED SHRIMP

4 pounds shrimp, fresh or frozen, 16 to 20 per pound
Pinch of each: salt, white pepper, cayenne pepper
1 lemon, halved

1. Be sure shrimp are thoroughly thawed. Place in heavy pot and cover with cold water.

2. Add salt, pepper, and both pieces of lemon and heat only to a boil. Remove from heat.

3. Immediately pour through a colander. Run cold water over the shrimp and peel and devein them while warm. Set aside.

SPINACH BASE

1 pound frozen spinach, thawed and cut into 1-inch squares
6 green onions, trimmed and chopped
1 bunch parsley, finely chopped
1 bunch celery, chopped medium
1 garlic clove, chopped
1 tablespoon salt
1 teaspoon white pepper
1 drop Tabasco sauce
3 tablespoons Worcestershire sauce
1/2 pound butter

1. Melt butter in heavy-bottomed pot.

2. Add drained spinach and simmer for 10 minutes.

3. Add all remaining ingredients, and simmer for about 1 hour, uncovered, stirring occasionally. Be sure that celery is cooked enough so that it is not crisp. Set aside.

CONTINUED...

MORNAY SAUCE

1/2 pound butter

3/4 cup all-purpose flour

1 quart milk, heated to boiling point

1 pound Swiss or Gruyère cheese, grated

Pinch cayenne pepper

1 teaspoon white pepper

3 ounces grated Parmesan cheese

1. Preheat oven to 425° F.

2. Make a roux*, melting butter and blending in flour over the heat. While blending in the flour, make sure the milk is very hot without boiling.

3. Take saucepan containing blended flour and butter off the heat and add the milk. Stir vigorously with a wire whip until roux is thickened. Place the saucepan back on high heat and continue stirring. As sauce thickens, add salt, pepper, cayenne pepper, and grated cheese.

4. Allow the sauce to come to a boil momentarily. Taste and adjust seasoning if necessary. Remove from heat immediately and pour into another container.

5. Cover the bottom of a 2- to 3-quart casserole with the spinach mixture. Lay all the shrimp over the spinach. Ladle the sauce over the shrimp and then sprinkle with grated Parmesan cheese, melted butter, and paprika.

6. Bake for 20 minutes.

*SEE GLOSSARY

SERVES: 8
PREPARATION TIME: 30 MINUTES
COOKING TIME: 1¾ HOURS

BOB HEILMAN'S BEACHCOMBER, CLEARWATER BEACH

Bimini Garlic Shrimp

Easy and so tasty. No matter how many shrimp you make, and no matter how many people there are, the shrimp will disappear! Another version of this is beer shrimp: instead of butter and garlic salt, use beer, salt, and pepper and prepare as above. This dish was a favorite of the locals for many years until the restaurant closed.

2 pounds shrimp, the largest you can find
Melted butter
Seasoned garlic salt to taste

1. Shell and devein the shrimp and arrange on an aluminum platter. Cover with melted butter and sprinkle generously with seasoned garlic salt.

2. Place under the broiler for a couple of minutes. Turn and broil on the other side. When shrimp are pink, they are ready to eat. Watch the shrimp closely so as not to overcook.

SERVES: 4
PREPARATION TIME: 5 TO 10 MINUTES
COOKING TIME: 5 TO 6 MINUTES

BIMINI SEA SHACK, FORT LAUDERDALE

Sarasota Pasta De Medici

There are just a few restaurants in Florida with more atmosphere than The Colony in Sarasota. While filming a special on the popular restaurant with a Tampa TV crew, we had to do "take" after "take". I was the only one who didn't seem to mind – I was able to sample this dish again and again and again! Wonderful spices and herbs combine to make this tutto bene!

1 pound fusili or other pasta, cooked al dente*, and slightly cooled
10 fresh jumbo shrimp, 10 to 15 per pound, cooked and sliced in half
2 ounces fresh chopped basil
2 ounces fresh rosemary
2 ounces fresh chopped chives
2 ounces scallions cut on bias (cut in julienne*)
2 ounces zucchini cut on bias (cut in julienne)
2 ounces Westphalian ham or other flavorful ham, cut in julienne
2 ounces shallots, chopped
2 ounces garlic, chopped
Fresh grated Parmesan cheese to taste
1 cup extra virgin olive oil
1/4 cup lemon or lime juice
1/4 cup red wine vinegar

1. Combine all ingredients in a bowl and toss lightly.

* SEE GLOSSARY

SERVES: 4 TO 6
PREPARATION TIME: 15 MINUTES
COOKING TIME: 10 MINUTES

THE COLONY RESTAURANT, LONGBOAT KEY

The Forge's Shrimp Merlin

The divergent sweet and sour taste of this very famous dish is intriguing. Garnished with cherry tomatoes and chopped parsley or fruits if you desire.

3 pounds large raw shrimp, shelled and deveined
3 quarts water
1 tablespoon thyme
1/2 teaspoon basil
4 hard-cooked egg yolks
4 tablespoons dry white wine vinegar
2 to 3 tablespoons sugar or more to taste
1 teaspoon dry mustard
1/4 teaspoon black pepper
2 1/2 cups mayonnaise
4 ounces capers, drained
2 medium onions, very thinly sliced
1/2 cup whipped heavy cream
1/2 cup sour cream, whipped until smooth
Lettuce for garnish

1. Bring water to boil in a large, heavy pot. Add thyme, basil, and shrimp. Bring to boil again, reduce heat, and simmer for 4 to 5 minutes, or until just done and shrimp is pink. Drain and cool completely.

2. Press 4 egg yolks through sieve into a large bowl. Add vinegar, sugar, mustard, pepper, and mayonnaise. Blend well.

3. Add capers, onions, and shrimp. Blend well again.

4. Fold in whipped cream and sour cream. Taste for seasoning. You may wish to add more pepper and a dash of salt.

To serve, place in lettuce cups and garnish as you wish.

SERVES: 6 TO 8 AS ENTRÉE, SALAD OR FIRST COURSE
PREPARATION TIME: 25 MINUTES, PLUS TIME FOR CHILLING
COOKING TIME: 5 MINUTES

THE FORGE, MIAMI BEACH

Shrimp Louis

Shrimp Louis is served at Joe's only at lunch. It's a most refreshing salad with a great distinctive flavor. JoAnn Bass, Joe's granddaughter, runs the restaurant today with her savvy son, Steve Sewitz. Needless to say, it's a winning duo.

SALAD

4 cups fresh or frozen cooked shrimp, 70 to 90 per pound size
16 leaves, leaf lettuce
4 cups shredded iceberg lettuce
2 tomatoes, quartered
4 hard-boiled eggs
8 pitted black olives
2 cups chick peas
4 green pepper rings
Shrimp Louis Dressing

1. On large platter, place 16 leaves of leaf lettuce. Cover center of platter with shredded iceberg.

2. Top with shrimp.

3. Garnish rest of dish with the remaining ingredients. Top with Shrimp Louis Dressing.

SHRIMP LOUIS DRESSING

1 cup mayonnaise
1 1/2 cups chili sauce
1/4 green pepper, chopped
1 to 2 tablespoons chopped pimiento
Paprika
Salt and pepper to taste
1/4 teaspoon dry mustard
1 tablespoon chopped onion
Dash Tabasco sauce
1/4 teaspoon horseradish

1. Mix above ingredients together well.

2. Chill thoroughly. Makes 2 1/2 cups, enough for 2 to 4 servings.

SERVES: 2 TO 4
PREPARATION TIME: 25 MINUTES

JOE'S STONE CRAB RESTAURANT, MIAMI BEACH

Shrimp Suzanne with Dill

A visit to the European-style Chalet Suzanne Resort and Restaurant is a must for aficionados of fine cuisine. If you prefer, land your private plane at the Chalet's private landing strip.

This shrimp salad is one of my favorites, especially when prepared by owner Vita Hinshaw!

1 pound, 25 to 30 count shrimp, cooked, peeled, and cleaned
1/2 cup sour cream
1/2 cup mayonnaise
1/2 fresh cucumber, seeded and scraped with spoon
1/2 cup finely chopped onions
1 1/2 tablespoons fresh chopped dill
1 1/2 teaspoons lemon juice
1/2 teaspoon garlic salt
1/4 teaspoon fresh ground pepper
1/4 teaspoon or about 8 drops Tabasco sauce
1/4 teaspoon caraway seed

1. Mix all ingredients, except shrimp, well. Add shrimp. Chill.

2. Serve on a bed of Bibb lettuce, either as individual servings or in lettuce-lined bowls.

SERVES: 4 TO 6
PREPARATION TIME: 15 MINUTES

CHALET SUZANNE, LAKE WALES

Derby Lane's Shrimp Mousse

This is a very rich dish, perfect for a first course. As a main course, serve with garden salad with a mild dressing. Pungent dressings will overpower the delicate shrimp flavor of the mousse. This appetizer dish may "rest" for a while, keeping warm, while you prepare the rest of the meal.

1 pound shrimp, raw, shelled, deveined
2 egg whites
2 cups heavy cream
1 1/2 teaspoon salt
1/2 teaspoon white pepper
1/4 teaspoon nutmeg
Shrimp Sauce (see recipe, page 250)

1. Preheat oven to 350° F.

2. Combine egg whites, heavy cream, salt, pepper, and nutmeg in a small bowl. Pour one third of mixture into the container of a blender or food processor. Add one-third pound of the shrimp. Blend into the consistency of a smooth paste, scraping the sides once or twice. Pour into a large mixing bowl. Repeat process until all ingredients are used. .

3. Pour mixture into a fancy 1-quart mold. A fish shape would be perfect. Place mold in a pan of tepid water. Cover with aluminum foil and bake for about 40 minutes.

4. Remove from oven and allow to rest for 5 minutes. Loosen edges; turn out onto serving platter and cover with Shrimp Sauce on page 259.

SERVES: 4 TO 6
PREPARATION TIME: 30 MINUTES
COOKING TIME: 40 MINUTES

DERBY LANE RESTAURANT, ST. PETERSBURG

Scampi Americana

This is super easy and quick if you have the brown sauce on hand. Villa Nova was a popular restaurant on the outskirts of Orlando. The restaurant closed, but I still often make this recipe given to me by the Italian owners.

2¹/₂ pounds jumbo shrimp, 6 to 8 shrimp per pound, peeled and deveined, shells reserved
1 cup all-purpose flour
3 tablespoons chopped scallions
1 tablespoon capers
3 ounces clarified butter*
2 ounces dry white wine
Juice of 1 lemon
4 ounces reduced* shrimp stock made from water and reserved shells
2 ounces light brown veal sauce*
3 ounces garlic butter*
Salt and cracked pepper
White rice or rice pilaf

1. Butterfly* the shrimp.

2. Melt the clarified butter in a large skillet. Dust the shrimp with flour and sauté until light brown. Add scallions and capers, and sauté for one minute. Add dry white wine, lemon juice, shrimp stock, and brown sauce. Let simmer.

3. Place shrimp atop rice pilaf.

4. Reduce* sauce in skillet until somewhat thick. Season with salt and cracked black pepper to taste to taste. Whisk in the garlic butter and pour over shrimp. Garnish with fresh parsley.

* SEE GLOSSARY

SERVES: 4
PREPARATION TIME: 20 MINUTES
COOKING TIME: 10 MINUTES

VILLA NOVA, WINTER PARK

Derby Lane's Baked Scampi

It's fun to bet on the dogs, but I'd rather share these leftovers with them. Here's the recipe as given to me by the manager of the once very fancy Derby Club.

2 pounds raw shrimp, 21 to 25 per pound, peeled, leaving the shell on the tail
1/2 pound butter
2 tablespoons Dijon mustard
1 tablespoon fresh lemon juice
1 tablespoon chopped garlic
1 tablespoon chopped parsley
Garnish of parsley sprigs and lemon wedges

1. Combine all the ingredients except the shrimp in a small saucepan, and heat over low heat for about 10 minutes.

2. Arrange shrimp in a shallow baking dish. Pour butter mixture over shrimp.

3. Bake at 450° F. for about 12 to 15 minutes, or until the shrimp lose their translucent look.

4. Garnish with parsley and lemon wedges.

SERVES: 6
PREPARATION TIME: 30 MINUTES, INCLUDING SHELLING
COOKING TIME: 25 MINUTES

DERBY LANE RESTAURANT, ST. PETERSBURG

Maison & Jardin Scampi Provençale

An elegant touch would be to serve this dish with a combination of white and wild rice. Taste this and you're in the south of France! If you don't wish to go that far, Altamonte Springs is a heartbeat from Orlando.

30 medium to large shrimp, peeled and sliced lengthwise
1/8 cup butter or extra virgin olive oil
3 cloves garlic, minced
2 cups sliced mushrooms
1/2 cup thinly sliced zucchini
5 tomatoes, seeded, peeled and diced
1 cup or less dry white wine
Rice

1. Lightly sauté the garlic in the butter or extra virgin olive oil.

2. Add shrimp and sauté until halfway cooked. Add mushrooms and zucchini and sauté 2 minutes. Add tomatoes. When ingredients are tender, add wine and simmer 2 minutes.

3. Serve over your favorite rice recipe.

SERVES: 6
PREPARATION TIME: 20 MINUTES
COOKING TIME: 10 MINUTES

MAISON & JARDIN RESTAURANT, ALTAMONTE SPRINGS

Shrimp Scampi Raintree

This is an easy but excellent recipe. Serve with asparagus or broccoli and a sliced tomato salad for a good interplay of taste and texture.

1¹/₂ pounds jumbo shrimp, peeled and deveined
1 pound sweet butter, well chilled and cut in large slices, or extra virgin olive oil
4 cloves garlic
2 tablespoons chopped parsley
Extra virgin olive oil for sautéing
1 pound mushrooms, quartered
1 cup dry white wine
1 tablespoon lemon juice
2 ounces Parmesan cheese
1 pint heavy cream
1 pound cooked buttered noodles

1. In the container of a food processor: combine butter or extra virgin olive oil, garlic, and parsley, and blend until smooth, about 1 minute.

2. Heat oil in a large skillet. Add mushrooms and swirl them in the oil. Add shrimp and cook over high heat for 30 seconds, stirring constantly. Reduce heat slightly and pour off excess oil. Leave a slight film of oil in the pan.

3. Whisk in wine, lemon juice, Parmesan, then cream. Continue cooking for about 1 minute or until the cream has reduced* slightly. Add butter-garlic-parsley combination. Reduce heat a little more and continue cooking for 3 or 4 minutes until the butter or oil mixture is incorporated, and the sauce has a shiny appearance.

4. Serve over the hot noodles.

* SEE GLOSSARY

SERVES: 4
PREPARATION TIME: 15 MINUTES
COOKING TIME: 10 MINUTES, PLUS THE NOODLES—OR START COOKING THE
NOODLES RIGHT AFTER STARTING THE MUSHROOMS

RAINTREE RESTAURANT, ST. AUGUSTINE

Shrimp Genovese

Having lived in Rome, Italy, as a student, I can attest to the authenticity of this *magnifico* recipe, which makes a delicious appetizer. You can add a little chopped red pepper if you like.

2 pounds large raw shrimp, shelled and deveined

MARINADE
2 cups extra virgin olive oil
1/2 cup red wine vinegar
1 cup dry white wine, Rhine or Sauterne suggested
3 cloves garlic, mashed
1 teaspoon basil, fresh is nice if available
1/4 teaspoon thyme
1 bay leaf, broken into pieces
1 clove, crushed
1 teaspoon onion powder
1 lemon, juiced, seeded and cut into pieces

1. Mix all marinade ingredients. Blend well. Add shrimp and marinate 3 to 4 hours.

2. Drain shrimp of marinade, then broil 2 or 3 minutes. Do not overcook. Marinade cooks the shrimp slightly to begin with.

SERVES: 6 TO 8 AS APPETIZER
PREPARATION TIME: 15 MINUTES
COOKING TIME: 2 TO 3 MINUTES
MARINATE: 3 TO 4 HOURS

ROLLANDE ET PIERRE, ST. PETERSBURG

Marty's Coconut Shrimp

The chef served this in the tradition of the Hana-Maui in Hawaii – with a tangy mustard fruit sauce, using the famous mustard fruits from Cremona, Italy, pineapple garnish, and white potato.

20 shrimp, 16 to 20 to a pound size, shelled and deveined
1 cup all-purpose flour
1¹/₂ cups milk mixed with 4 eggs, slightly beaten
¹/₂ cup shredded coconut
2 tablespoons Coconut Amaretto liqueur or Amaretto liqueur
4 pineapple rings for garnish
Mustard Fruit Sauce (see recipe, page 264)

1. Butterfly* shrimp.

2. Dust shrimp in flour, then dip in egg-milk combination. Roll shrimp in shredded coconut and deep fry until golden brown. Sprinkle with coconut. Lightly sprinkle with Coconut Amaretto.

3. Garnish plate with pineapple rings. Serve with a soufflé cup (¹/₂ cup) of warmed Mustard Fruit Sauce.

* SEE GLOSSARY

SERVES: 1
PREPARATION TIME: 5 MINUTES
COOKING TIME: 2 TO 4 MINUTES

MARTY'S STEAKS, TAMPA

Columbia Shrimp Supreme

Richard Gonzmart, owner of The Columbia Restaurants with his brother Casey and mother Adela, gave me this very famous recipe prepared originally at the Ybor City restaurant, only one of many Columbia Restaurants. Try it. You can't eat just one!

16 jumbo shrimp, peeled and deveined, and tail left on
Juice of one lemon
1 teaspoon garlic powder
1 teaspoon salt
1/2 teaspoon pepper
8 strips of bacon
Toothpicks
2 eggs, lightly beaten
1/2 cup milk
All-purpose flour

1. Pat shrimp dry. Marinate in lemon juice, garlic powder, salt, and pepper for 10 minutes.

2. Cut bacon strips in half, wrap around shrimp and secure with a toothpick.

3. Beat together eggs and milk, and dip shrimp in batter. Roll into all-purpose flour.

4. Deep fry at 300° F. until golden brown, about 5 to 8 minutes.

SERVES: 4 AS AN APPETIZER
PREPARATION TIME: 15 MINUTES
COOKING TIME: 5 MINUTES

THE COLUMBIA RESTAURANTS, TAMPA, SARASOTA,
ST. PETERSBURG, AND ST. AUGUSTINE

Joe's Shrimp Creole

This is a Floridian version of Creole that is quite good. And you thought that Joe's had only great stone crabs!

2 pounds shrimp, peeled, deveined and cooked
1/2 cup chopped celery
1/2 cup chopped onion
1/4 cup chopped salt pork or may use bacon
1 2 1/2-pound can tomatoes
3/4 cup chili sauce
1/4 cup tomato paste
1/2 teaspoon thyme
1 teaspoon Maggi® seasoning
2 cloves garlic, finely chopped
Salt and pepper to taste
Cooked rice

1. Simmer celery, onions, and salt pork or bacon until cooked. Add all the other ingredients except the shrimp.

2. Cook for 30 minutes over a low heat.

3. Add shrimp and warm through.

4. Serve over rice.

SERVES: 4 TO 6
PREPARATION TIME: 15 MINUTES
COOKING TIME: 45 MINUTES

JOE'S STONE CRAB RESTAURANT, MIAMI BEACH

Park Plaza Shrimp Curry

Curry is a mixture of at least 13 different spices. This popular dish can be made with an Indian curry as well as with an island curry such as Blue Mountain®, one of my favorites from the Caribbean island of Jamaica!

CURRY SAUCE

- 3 tablespoons clarified butter*
- 4 cloves garlic, chopped
- 3 ribs celery, chopped
- 1 large peeled carrot, chopped
- 2 medium onions, chopped
- 1 bunch parsley, chopped (stems removed)
- 2 ounces good curry powder
- 1 3/4 quarts chicken velouté sauce*
- 1/2 cup dry white wine
- 2 medium tomatoes, peeled, seeded, and chopped
- Juice and rind of 2 large oranges
- 1/2 teaspoon of mace
- 1/2 teaspoon of cloves
- 1/2 teaspoon of cayenne pepper
- 1/2 teaspoon of coriander
- 1/2 teaspoon of ginger
- 1/2 teaspoon of white pepper
- 3/4 teaspoon of cinnamon
- 3/4 teaspoon of allspice
- 1 1/2 cups heavy cream
- Salt to taste

1. Gently sauté garlic, celery, peeled carrot, and onion in 3 tablespoons of the clarified butter for about 5 minutes. Add parsley and curry powder.

2. When curry powder turns light brown, add the dry white wine and chicken velouté sauce.

3. Simmer for 5 minutes and then add the remaining ingredients except the salt.

4. Simmer for 30 to 45 minutes, strain, and add salt to taste.

* SEE GLOSSARY

CONTINUED...

SHRIMP

3 pounds jumbo shrimp, peeled and deveined
3/4 pound clarified butter*
3 Red Delicious apples, peeled, cored, and cut in julienne*
1 1/4 cups mango chutney
6 hard-cooked egg yolks, grated
1 cup currants
1 cup toasted coconut, shredded

1. Butterfly* the shrimp and sauté in 6 ounces of hot clarified butter.

2. When shrimp just begin to cook, add the curry sauce and simmer for 5 minutes. Add apples and remove from heat.

3. Serve on timbales of rice pilaf and accompany with chutney, yolks, currants, and toasted coconut.

RICE PILAF

2 tablespoons butter
1 small onion, diced
1 ribs celery, diced
2 cups Uncle Ben's Converted rice
4 cups well-seasoned chicken stock
2 crushed bay leaves

1. Sauté the onion and celery rib in 2 tablespoons of melted butter.

2. When onion turns golden, stir in the rice, making sure that it is well coated with the butter.

3. Add chicken stock and bring to boil. Add crushed bay leaves and simmer 20 to 25 minutes until done.

* SEE GLOSSARY

SERVES: 6
PREPARATION TIME: 30 MINUTES
COOKING TIME: APPROXIMATELY 45 MINUTES, NOT INCLUDING RICE

PARK PLAZA GARDENS, WINTER PARK

Shrimp Lauren

This is a remarkably delectable dish if you are trying to save on calories or just love shrimp. The fresh ingredients make a beautiful presentation.

1¹/2 pounds large shrimp, cooked**
¹/2 cup butter
¹/2 cup extra virgin olive oil
Salt and pepper to taste
3 to 4 cloves garlic, slightly mashed
1 stalk celery, peeled and coarsely chopped
1 large onion, minced
4 green peppers, cut in ³/4-inch squares
¹/4 cup lemon juice
1 pound tomatoes, coarsely chopped

1. In a large heavy skillet melt butter. Add extra virgin olive oil, salt and pepper. Add garlic and sauté until soft. Add celery. Cook covered until celery softens.

2. Add onion and green peppers. Cook, stirring frequently, until vegetables are nearly done and still crunchy. Stir in lemon juice and remove from heat.

3. Add tomatoes after contents of pan cools. Cover for a few minutes and continue to cool.

4. If serving immediately, add the shrimp, mix well, and serve. Garnish with parsley.

NOTE: IF PREPARING AHEAD, LET COOL AND STORE UNTIL SERVING TIME. AT TIME OF SERVICE, PLACE INTO INDIVIDUAL CASSEROLES OR LARGE CASSEROLE. ADD PREPARED SHELLFISH AND PLACE IN OVEN UNTIL HOT. SERVE.

** ALSO GREAT WITH SCALLOPS

SERVES: 6 TO 8
PREPARATION TIME: 15 MINUTES
COOKING TIME: 15 MINUTES

SIPLE'S GARDEN SEAT, CLEARWATER

Pier House Shrimp Curaçao

Lovely looking and delicious tasting. An unusual way to prepare shrimp.

24 large raw shrimp, peeled and deveined
2 oranges, squeezed and peel reserved
2 cups hollandaise sauce*
Salt and pepper to taste
6 tablespoons clarified butter*
1/2 cup orange curaçao**
4 cups wild rice pilaf, prepared as you wish
1 cup whipped cream
2 bunches watercress for garnish

1. Cut zest from orange into very fine julienne*. Blanch* and cool.

2. Prepare hollandaise sauce and add juice from squeezed orange. Keep warm.

3. Season shrimp with salt and cracked black pepper to taste. Heat butter in large heavy skillet. Sauté shrimp 2 to 3 minutes or until just tender. Carefully flambé* with warmed curaçao.

4. Reduce* cooking liquid in pan about 2 minutes. Do not overcook shrimp.

5. To serve, arrange shrimp in a row over two individual servings of rice. Nap* with orange hollandaise. Top with a dollop of whipped cream, sprinkle with orange julienne, and garnish with watercress.

** DO NOT SUBSTITUTE LOWER PROOF LIQUEUR: IT WILL NOT FLAME

* SEE GLOSSARY

SERVES: 4
PREPARATION TIME: 30 TO 35 MINUTES
COOKING TIME: 6 MINUTES PLUS TIME FOR HOLLANDAISE SAUCE AND RICE

THE PIER HOUSE, KEY WEST

The Lobster Pot's Hawaiian Shrimp With Sherry Sauce

This is attractive to serve, and it draws raves. Be sure to get the bacon crisp and do not overcook the shrimp.

SHRIMP

12 large shrimp, shelled and deveined, shells reserved
1 teaspoon garlic salt
Juice of 1/2 lemon
12 small slices of fresh or canned pineapple
1 green bell pepper, cut into 12 strips
6 slices bacon, cut in half and blanched*
Toothpicks
1/2 cup pineapple juice
6 tablespoons melted butter

1. Marinate shrimp in a non-metallic bowl in garlic salt and lemon mixture for 10 minutes.

2. Wrap a shrimp, a pineapple piece, and a green pepper strip with a strip of bacon. Secure with toothpick. Pour pineapple juice over all. Marinate one hour in refrigerator.

* SEE GLOSSARY

CONTINUED...

SHERRY SAUCE

Shells from shelled shrimp
1 cup water
5 black peppercorns
2 crushed bay leaves
1 cup sweet sherry
3 tablespoons coarsely chopped onion
1/4 cup butter
1/4 cup all-purpose flour
1/3 cup heavy cream
4 tablespoons Parmesan cheese
Salt and white pepper to taste
Dash Worcestershire sauce

1. Make stock by combining shrimp shells, water, peppercorns, crushed bay leaves, sherry, and onions. Bring to a boil and simmer 10 minutes. Strain through cheesecloth.

2. Preheat oven to 400° F.

3. Melt butter for sauce in a pan. Add flour and stir until blended and bubbling. Stir in stock and carefully whisk in cream. Add Parmesan, salt, white pepper, and Worcestershire sauce, stirring until smooth. Keep warm.

4. Arrange shrimp in a shallow baking pan, drizzle with melted butter, and bake for about 7 minutes. To serve, place on 2 small plates and top with warmed sherry sauce. Do not simmer shrimp in sauce; they will overcook.

SERVES: 4 AS AN APPETIZER
PREPARATION TIME: 20 MINUTES PLUS 1 HOUR, 10 MINUTES FOR MARINATING
COOKING TIME: 30 MINUTES

THE LOBSTER POT, REDINGTON SHORES

Pappas' Peppered Shrimp Appetizer

Louis Pappas, Jr., now owns and runs this successful waterside restaurant in Tarpon Springs. Louis is a bona fide chef himself and takes pride in his new creations, including his own private label extra virgin olive oil. Be sure to try this easy to prepare dish at home or on the boat if you can't make it to Pappas'.

12 large shrimp, unshelled
1/2 cup extra virgin olive oil
1 1/2 cloves garlic, finely chopped
2 tablespoons lemon juice
2 tablespoons lime juice
2 ounces dry vermouth
1 teaspoon salt
1 tablespoon coarse pepper
Lemon and lime slices for garnish

1. Heat oil to 375° F. and slightly sauté garlic until brown.

2. Add rest of ingredients and sauté until shrimp are pink and slightly firm, about 5 to 10 minutes. Stir occasionally. Remove most of liquid.

3. Serve garnished with lemon and lime slices and some pan juices.

SERVES: 4 AS AN APPETIZER
PREPARATION TIME: 5 MINUTES
COOKING TIME: 5 TO 10 MINUTES

LOUIS PAPPAS' RIVERSIDE RESTAURANT, TARPON SPRINGS

Clearwater Shrimp Moutarde

This is easy to make and quite tasty! Another serving suggestion is to double the sauce recipe, add 2 to 3 tablespoons of milk to thin slightly, add shrimp. Place all in casserole dish and bake for 15 to 20 minutes. Serve over rice.

20 large shrimp, peeled, deveined, and cooked
¹/₄ cup mayonnaise
1 to 2 tablespoons Dijon mustard
2 tablespoons minced onion
³/₄ cup finely chopped celery
Croutons for garnish

1. Preheat oven to 350° F.

2. Combine mayonnaise, mustard, onion, and celery. Place one-fourth in each of 4 ramekins. Add 5 shrimp to each ramekin. Top with croutons and bake for 8 to 10 minutes. Serve immediately.

* SEE GLOSSARY

SERVES: 4
PREPARATION TIME: 20 MINUTES
COOKING TIME: 8 TO 20 MINUTES

SIPLE'S GARDEN SEAT, CLEARWATER

Pepin's Shrimp Almendrina

I have lived in St. Petersburg since 1975 with a 6-year stint on Miami Beach during that time. For all of those years I have always been able to order this extraordinary dish at Pepin's, a Spanish-style restaurant on Fourth Street. It is always delicious! You'll love the sauce. This recipe is a must for your cooking repertoire. This is one of our favorite shrimp dishes.

2¹/₂ pounds jumbo shrimp, peeled and deveined, tails intact
2 eggs
2 cups milk
2 cups all-purpose flour
Salt and cracked black pepper
4 cups sliced almonds
Oil for deep-frying
Orange Mustard Sauce or other fruit sauce for dipping (see recipe, page 261)

1. Beat the eggs until light and fluffy in medium-size non-metallic bowl. Stir in milk. Gradually add flour, blending well. Add salt and cracked black pepper to taste.

2. Hold shrimp by tail and dip into batter, allowing excess to drip back into bowl. Do not cover tails with batter. Sprinkle all sides of batter-coated shrimp with almonds. Place on cookie sheet and refrigerate at least 2 hours before frying.

3. Heat oil to 375° F. Deep fry shrimp a few at a time, just until they turn pink, about 2 minutes. Do not overcook.

4. Drain on paper towels and keep warm until all shrimp have been cooked.

5. Serve immediately with Orange Mustard Sauce on 261.

SERVES: 6 TO 8
PREPARATION TIME: 20 MINUTES PLUS TIME FOR CHILLING
COOKING TIME: 2 MINUTES EACH BATCH

PEPIN'S, ST. PETERSBURG

Selena's Shrimp Manales

The sauce is so delicious and abundant, be sure to serve with rice or over pasta. If you serve it over pasta, this recipe could serve up to 10 people. One tablespoon black pepper is correct!

3 pounds medium-sized shrimp, peeled and deveined
1 tablespoon black pepper
1/2 tablespoon salt
1/2 tablespoon white pepper
1/2 pound margarine, melted
1/2 pound butter, melted
2 ounces Worcestershire sauce
1 1/2 tablespoons finely chopped garlic
1/2 cup lemon juice

1. Preheat oven to 350° F.

2. Combine all of the ingredients except shrimp and mix well.

3. Place shrimp in casserole dish and stir in the mixture.

4. Bake for 15 to 20 minutes or until shrimp are done. Do not overcook.

SERVES: 6
PREPARATION TIME: 30 MINUTES
COOKING TIME: 15 TO 20 MINUTES

SELENA'S, TAMPA

LOBSTER
LOVER

Lobster

Oh...How Things Change

These underwater "bugs," as they are affectionately called in the Keys and the Caribbean islands, were once treated along the same lines as their insect nickname-sakes. Early North American settlers used them as fertilizer, as fish bait, and as food for servants of the rich because they were so abundant.

But diners soon realized they were sacrificing a delicious meat, and commercial lobstering took hold in the 1800s, a tight hold. Though there are now rules to protect lobster, rampant harvesting has put a squeeze on today's population, driving cost—and the status of now-cherished lobster—way up.

Pinch Me

Though there are many more species nearby, Americans basically have access to two kinds of lobster: those with claws, found mainly in northern United States waters, and the spiny lobsters without claws, which are found in southern waters and in the Caribbean (elsewhere, too).

The northern species (American or Maine lobster) have sweeter, softer meat than do their southern counterparts. But despite the different tastes, both have virtually the same nutritional value. Each is low in fat, a good source of vitamins and minerals, and not as high in cholesterol as once thought. Four ounces of lobster measure up to be only ninety-some calories, 1.5 grams of fat, and about 120 milligrams of cholesterol.

A Hard (and Soft) Life

The spiny lobster—also called Florida lobster, rock lobster, and Caribbean lobster, among others—is named for its numerous spines on its adult body. Other characteristics: a hooked horn over each eye, a pair of long antennae, ten legs, a segmented tail, and a reddish-brown shade mottled with yellow, orange, green, and blue and creamy spots.

The journey to this adult form is a long and difficult one for the spiny lobster. Perhaps the least of its worries—at least early on—is man. Though an average-sized female spiny lobster (five or six inches in these parts) can hatch as many two hundred and fifty thousand to more than one million eggs, only a few of these lobsters probably will survive predators, other lobsters included, to become adults. Thanks to us, even fewer will grow close to reaching their potential of more than one and a half feet.

The danger is especially grave when the lobster is most vulnerable, both early in its life and during each of its many molts, when the lobster sheds its tough (but forever-not-big-enough) shell to make room for a more accommodating replacement. During this transition, its body stays soft and unprotected.

Between a Rock and a Hard Place

During the juvenile and adult molts, spiny lobsters hole up in dens on rocky or camouflaged bottoms not too far from a coast. Actually, no matter what shell they are or aren't sporting, they spend every daylight hour here, only coming out to eat under the safety of night. The bigger lobsters stay in deeper water; the smaller ones keep to shallow depths.

What they haven't figured out yet is now that we know where to look for them, their hiding places aren't all that impressive. Especially when you consider that several lobsters pack into the same hole, and each leaves its antennae sticking out, a sure come-and-get-me sign to lobster-seeking divers.

Commercial fishermen have it even easier. They drop slatted wooden crates to the bottom of the ocean floor, and lobster, thinking the box would be a good den for the day, climb right through the open hole in the top. Only a few good lobsters (usually the smaller, more agile ones) will escape.

But laws protect the dwindled spiny lobster family now. Catch has to be a certain size and has to be taken with certain gear. There are also limits to how many can be bagged and during which months they can be captured. Today's season allows you to hunt from August through March. A two-day sport season is also available near the end of July. That's when I head to Key West for a few days of great eats!

Fairy "Tails"

Because the southern spiny lobsters store all of their usable meat in their tails (remember, they have no claws), this species is most often sold just as that: lobster tails. Some markets figure they will spare you the hassle of dismantling whole lobsters just to get to the tail meat; others know there is a much larger demand for Maine lobster, though the deliciousness of each is a constant debate.

The tails can be raw and fresh (or "green") during season, raw and frozen, or cooked and sold fresh or frozen. Most of these will include shells, for good reason. The tail shells will prevent the meat from drying out and losing taste.

Just make sure, as is the case with any seafood, that the lobster tails smell fresh and sea-like, not fishy.

Raw meat should be soft and look translucent. Tails, frozen or fresh, should not have black spots on them, a sign of aging. Frozen tails–which might be your only option during lobsters' off months–should also be solid, with no signs of thawing in the form of ice crystals.

Cooked meat in the shell should be white and firm with a red outer membrane, and the shells, whether frozen or ready to serve, should have turned a bright red-orange. Meat and shell should be attached tightly.

What's sometimes referred to as "picked meat", meat taken out of the shell, also should be white and firm and clean smelling. The membrane may or may not be a part of your buy since it turns tough.

Iced or Tanked

The best way to buy northern lobsters is whole and fresh because they offer more meat that way and of course, the fresher, the better. But make sure they're more than just alive. See that they're lively.

Those in a tank may have been in the same water for longer than they should have been, rapidly losing spirit and taste. Try this trick (but first make sure their claws are strapped or pegged): Pick one up. If it doesn't splay or flip its tail and legs in an attempt to free itself, you free it, and grab another. Or touch its eyes, and see if the lobster twitches. Check out the tail, too, which should tend to tuck underneath the body. (I suggest you let the owner know what you're up to).

Live lobsters can also be stored in the market on ice. Some chefs even prefer to buy them this way. Because lobsters don't live as long on ice as they do in storage tanks, these cooks rationalize that lobsters on ice are fresher.

Notice the feel of the shell when you pick up the northern lobster. Those that had not finished molting when they were pulled from the sea will feel soft. These soft-shell lobsters, or shedders, have less meat than do equal-sized hard-shells. You can cook lobster in either stage, but you won't get the same servings out of them, possibly not even the same taste. The softer the meat, the more loose and watery it is, sweeter too.

While you're holding din-din, take a look at the lobster's underside to determine its sex. Females, which supposedly offer more meat, have two soft swimmerets near the spot where the tail meets the body; male's swimmerets are hard.

As far as size, you probably won't have that much of a choice. Most will be about one and a half pounds or so. The bigger, the easier it is to get to the meat; the smaller, some say, the more tender, but that is not always true. I have eaten lobsters up to eight pounds that were every bit as delicious as any smaller ones I've tasted.

Fill 'er Up

How many lobsters per person? On average: a tail (both sides) or two of spiny lobsters or a single one-and-a-half-pound whole northern or spiny lobster.

When serving lobster in a dish, about one pound raw lobster in the shell will give you about one-third cooked lobster meat.

Keepers

Simply put, fresh raw tails and live lobster should be kept in the coldest part of the refrigerator and cooked quickly. Try to keep the whole lobster alive, in fact, in an open container covered with a damp towel until the minute you are ready to cook. Some may last a few hours to much more, but you never know.

Or you can buy lobster tails frozen or freeze whole lobster live if need be, and they will keep about four months—provided they are well protected. To thaw, set in the refrigerator for a good while or run (still encapsulated) under cold running water. The red outer membrane may have to be removed before serving the lobster, because freezing can make it too tough to enjoy.

Cooked lobster will be okay in the refrigerator about two or three days, but it's not best to freeze it. You'll be disappointed with the texture and taste. Use it for lobster salad; you will have arrived!

Finally, for the Finale

Lobster tails can be broiled, grilled, steamed, fried, or boiled. (There are no losers in the debate about boiling them in saltwater or in salted water; either seems to work fine.) Add seaweed for more flavor.

To cook the tails (except boiling), you'll need to clean them first and then butterfly them. To butterfly lobster tails, cut lengthwise with a very sharp knife down the top of the tail, from tip to fan. Don't cut the bottom shell. Just spread the two still-attached topsides open until the bottom shell snaps and the sides will sit down.

Cooked meat should be white and firm and the shells a bright orange-red. Be careful not to overcook these tails, or they'll dry out and not be worth the money you paid for them.

If you just need the meat for a mixed dish, cut the shells any old helter-skelter way and pull out as much meat as possible, which you will be able to cook any number of ways.

Cooking northern lobsters is a bit trickier and more involved. For one, they're still alive; two, they're whole. But if that's the way you want to go, ask your fish dealer for directions. If you're really a softy, you could ask the dealer to kill the lobsters for you, but remember that the less time between killing them and cooking them, the better.

Brothers' Blue Lagoon Lobster Salad

Bring a light touch of the tropics to your next dinner party with this delectable recipe made with a great combination: lobster, tropical fruit, and kiwi.

2 cups cooked lobster
2 ripe pineapples
2/3 cup diced celery
1/2 cup macadamia nuts
1/4 cup shredded coconut
1/3 cup mayonnaise
1/4 cup diced kiwi fruit or white seedless grapes
Additional kiwi for garnish

1. Drain and cut lobster into bite-size pieces.

2. Cut pineapple in half lengthwise. Remove fruit from each half and save shells. Cut pineapple into chunks.

3. Combine lobster, pineapple chunks, celery, macadamia nuts, coconut, mayonnaise, and kiwi fruit. Fill the pineapple halves with mixture and garnish with sliced kiwi. White seedless grapes can be substituted for kiwi.

SERVES: 4
PREPARATION TIME: 15 MINUTES
COOKING TIME: 5 MINUTES

BROTHERS, TOO, TAMPA

Lobster Thermidor

Use any kind of lobster that is available for this classic '50s recipe. Canned mushrooms can be used – don't sauté – but fresh are better, of course.

2 1¼-pound Florida lobsters, split, cleaned, and rinsed
1 quart water
Salt to taste
2 crushed bay leaves
5 peppercorns
1 cup hollandaise sauce*

1. Poach the lobsters in the water, salt, crushed bay leaves, and peppercorns for about 5 minutes or until the lobster are cooked. Remove from water and reserve 2 cups of the poaching stock.

2. Dice the lobster and keep warm. Rinse out the shells and reserve.

S A U C E

3 ounces butter
2½ ounces all-purpose flour
1 cup Chablis or other dry white wine
2 cups reserved stock
1 cup sliced mushrooms, sautéed in 2 tablespoons of butter
½ cup Parmesan cheese
Salt and white pepper
½ teaspoon sugar
1 teaspoon Worcestershire sauce
1 teaspoon lemon juice

1. Melt the butter and stir in the flour to make a roux*. Cook and stir for 2 minutes. Gradually add the Chablis and reserved stock and cook, stirring, for 1 minute. Add the mushrooms, Parmesan, salt and white pepper to taste, sugar, Worcestershire, and lemon juice.

2. Line the lobster shells with the sauce. Divide the lobster meat up and place in shells. Top with more sauce.

3. Top with hollandaise sauce, about 2 to 3 tablespoons for each, and bake in 400° F. oven for 10 minutes.

* SEE GLOSSARY

SERVES: 2
PREPARATION TIME: 30 MINUTES
COOKING TIME: 20 MINUTES

THE LOBSTER POT, REDINGTON SHORES

Kyushu Lobster Tempura

The secret – keep the batter very cold and the oil very hot. This will give you that wonderfully light tempura as made at Kyushu. Try other seafood and vegetables as well with this batter. Use a wok because of its large surface area and slanted sides, which protect against splattering.

2 Florida or Maine lobster tails, about 1 pound.
2 eggs, beaten
3/4 cup white all-purpose flour
1 teaspoon sake (Japanese liqueur)
1 cup cold water or chopped ice
Vegetable oil for deep frying
Tempura sauce (see recipe, page 264)

1. Remove shell from lobster. Cut lobster into bite-size pieces. Wipe excess water off each piece. Set aside.

2. Heat oil to about 360° F. Be careful, as oil is very hot.

BATTER

1. To make batter, add eggs to flour. Mix in very cold water or ice. Kyushu adds ice to the batter to keep it very cold.

2. Add sake. Mix batter as little as possible, no more than 10 to 20 seconds.

3. Place bowl in water to keep batter very cold. Start mixing only after oil has heated up.

4. Dip lobster in flour, then in batter. Coat evenly and let excess batter drip off naturally before frying. Slip pieces gently into oil with tongs, fork, or chopsticks. Do not move it around until batter has cooked.

5. Continually skim the oil and pick up loose batter. Fry a few at a time until light brown.

6. Serve with Tempura Sauce (see recipe, page 264).

SERVES: 4
PREPARATION TIME: 15 MINUTES
COOKING TIME: 2 TO 3 MINUTES

KYUSHU RESTAURANT-SUSHI BAR, KEY WEST

Bernard's Lobster Buena Vista

If you use frozen lobster shells, completely defrost and pat dry before proceeding with the recipe. If you have hearty eaters, plan on 2 lobster tails per person. The dish is rich, so they might not eat it all, but the leftovers are heavenly!

4 8-ounce lobster tails with shells
2 to 3 quarts court-bouillon*
3 tablespoons butter
1 pound mushrooms, sliced
1/2 quart dry white wine
1/2 quart heavy cream
1 teaspoon chopped fresh thyme, or 1/2 teaspoon dried
1/4 pound butter
1/4 cup all-purpose flour
1 tablespoon lemon juice
Salt and cracked black pepper
2 dashes Worcestershire sauce, or to taste

1. Cook the lobster tails in court-bouillon* until done (turn white). Drain and reserve liquid.

2. Sauté the mushrooms in the 3 tablespoons butter until they have released all their juices and the pan is almost dry.

3. Bring 1/2 quart of court-bouillon, white wine, heavy cream, and thyme to a boil.

4. In the meantime, melt the 1/4 pound butter and stir about 1/4 cup all-purpose flour to make a roux*. Cook for 3 minutes and gradually whisk in the court-bouillon sauce. Bring to a boil, stirring constantly, then remove from the heat.

5. Remove lobster meat from the shells and dice. Mix the lobster meat with the sauce. Season to taste with salt and cracked black pepper to taste, Worcestershire, and lemon juice.

6. Pile mixture into the lobster shells and quickly heat under the broiler until golden.

* SEE GLOSSARY

SERVES: 4
PREPARATION TIME: 30 MINUTES
COOKING TIME: 30 MINUTES

BERNARD'S, BOYNTON BEACH

Peter's Lobster Thermidor

Peter Kersker, a good friend of mine, owned Peter's Place in downtown St. Petersburg. This was one of his best entrées.

The first step can be done earlier in the day and the lobster meat and shells refrigerated just until ready to cook. Florida lobsters have meat mostly in their tails and there's not enough to refill both the body and the tail. Feel free to use just the body or just the tail to stuff and serve.

1 Florida lobster or Maine lobster, split into halves
1 cup of béchamel sauce*
2 teaspoons chopped chives
1/2 stick butter or olive oil
2 tablespoons dry sherry
2 tablespoons brandy for flaming
1/4 cup grated Parmesan cheese, plus 1 tablespoon
1/4 cup heavy cream
4 paper-thin slices Swiss or Gruyère cheese
4 paper-thin slices Canadian bacon
Paprika

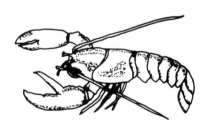

CONTINUED...

1. Remove lobster meat from lobsters after draining well. Squeeze the meat to remove excess moisture, then cut into bite-sized chunks.

2. Make the béchamel sauce* and keep warm.

3. Sauté the cut-up lobster in ¹/₄ stick melted butter or extra virgin olive oil. Add the chives. Flame* the lobster-butter-chive mixture with the brandy. Remove the lobster with a slotted spoon and place back into the lobster shells.

4. Add the butter-brandy-chive mixture to the béchamel sauce and heat. Add the other ¹/₄ stick butter or extra virgin olive oil and the sherry. Stir in the ¹/₄ cup of Parmesan, add the heavy cream, and whisk together well.

5. Pour the béchamel mixture all over, in, and around the lobster in the shells, reserving a few tablespoons of the sauce. Place 2 slices of Canadian bacon on each lobster half and 2 slices of the cheese on top of the Canadian bacon. Spread reserved béchamel on top of cheese and sprinkle with remaining Parmesan. Sprinkle paprika for color.

6. Bake for 20 minutes at 350° F. and serve.

* SEE GLOSSARY

SERVES: 4
PREPARATION TIME: 45 MINUTES
COOKING TIME: 20 MINUTES

PETER'S PLACE, ST. PETERSBURG

Lobster With Caviar

You can make the Fish Fumé and Nantua Sauce ahead and refrigerate.
Decadently delicious!

FISH FUMÉ

1 pound fish bones from snapper, sea bass, turbot, etc.
1/2 stalk celery
1/2 onion
1 1/2 large ripe tomatoes
1/2 bay leaf
Salt and whole black pepper to taste
1 pint cold water

1. Thinly slice celery, onion, and tomatoes. Place all the ingredients into a pot. Bring to boil and simmer for 30 minutes or long enough to reduce* it to one-third.

NANTUA SAUCE

2 tablespoons soybean oil
6 8-ounce lobster tails
2 ounces dry white wine
1 1/2 large tomatoes, diced
1 1/2 ounces brown roux*
1 pint Fish Fumé

1. Shell the lobster tails and set the meat aside.

2. Mix the lobster shells with the oil, wine, tomatoes, roux, and Fish Fumé. Cook over a medium heat for 20 minutes. Skim very often and strain.

* SEE GLOSSARY

CONTINUED...

LOBSTER

Meat from 6 lobster tails
1 ounce shallots, peeled and chopped
2 ounces cognac
2/3 cup Nantua Sauce (see recipe above)
1 1/2 ounces heavy cream
2 tablespoons soybean oil
1/2 ounce Beluga or other caviar

1. Cut lobster meat into medallions, 4 medallions per tail.

2. Sauté the shallots in the oil. Add the lobster medallions and cook until nearly done. Deglaze* with the cognac and flame*. Remove the lobster and set aside.

3. Add the Nantua Sauce to the pan. Bring to a boil, and add salt and black pepper to taste. Turn off the heat.

4. Place the lobster back into the pan with the sauce. Add the cream and top with the Beluga caviar. Serve.

* SEE GLOSSARY

SERVES: 6
PREPARATION TIME: 1 HOUR
COOKING TIME: 1 HOUR

KING CHARLES RESTAURANT AT THE DON CESAR HOTEL, ST. PETE BEACH

Lobster With Cognac

This recipe preserves the flavor of the lobster. *C'est magnifique!*

4 6- to 8-ounce lobster tails in shell
2 ounces melted butter
2 bulbs shallots, finely diced
2 ripe tomatoes
3 ounces cognac
Salt and white pepper to taste
4 ounces heavy cream
2 cups cooked rice

1. Remove lobster from shell and cut into small bite-size pieces.

2. Heat butter in a frying pan. Add shallots and lobster and sauté until lobster is halfway cooked. Add tomatoes to lobster.

3. Add cognac and carefully ignite with a match. Let flame extinguish by itself.

4. Add salt and pepper to taste. Add heavy cream and cook until lobster is done.

5. On each 10-inch dinner plate, place $1/2$ cup of cooked rice. Pour lobster mixture on top. Cover with sauce and serve with fresh vegetables.

SERVES: 4 TO 6
PREPARATION TIME: 10 MINUTES
COOKING TIME: 10 MINUTES

CHATEAU PARISIAN, TAMPA

CRAB DADDY

Crabs

Healthful Eating

They may try to intimidate you with their beady, little eyes, hunched attack positions, and I'm-going-to-get-you claws. But bad doesn't go to the bone (or cartilage) in these flavorfully sweet creatures. These tasty treats are a delight to eat. Some diners even seem to enjoy them more than they do lobster. (Can you imagine?)

And, like many other shellfish, they're much better for you than once believed. Though Florida markets have access to several different species (two of the best from waters right off our coasts), most crabs have about the same range of nutritional value: sixty to ninety calories, one to one and a half grams of fat (a lot of those beneficial omega-3s), and forty-five to eighty milligrams of cholesterol per three ounces, plus plenty of vitamin B, protein, zinc, calcium, and other important, funny-named stuff.

Not bad. In fact, we now know the cholesterol in crab is equal to that in a skinless chicken, often mistakenly considered the dieter's only option. But do watch out for the sodium content: 280 to 320 milligrams in that same three ounces.

Leftovers

Some may turn to the West Coast's large Dungeness crab for its full taste, the mammoth ten-pounder king crab from Alaskan waters for easy eating, or the Pacific's meaty-legged snow crab. But with the riches Florida has right in our back yard, it seems only logical to take advantage of our good fortune: the stone crab, blue crab (with hard and soft shells), and a late bloomer, golden crab.

Just a Stone's Throw Away

A brownish-red with shades of gray, stone crabs make early homes among the rocks and shells of bays and estuaries off the Atlantic and Gulf coasts. Grown-up and a little braver, they move to more shallow water, just below the line of low tide, and bury themselves in the sand in holes twelve to twenty inches deep.

They are easy to distinguish, with oval, hard bodies and two large claws. If you look a little closer, you'll see an even better identification: Inside the larger claw sits a pattern resembling a thumbprint.

Do get familiar with the claws. They are the only part of the stone crab Florida will allow you to eat, provided the claws are taken without harming the crab. And since stone crabs are commercially harvested almost exclusively in Florida, that's all you will see.

From mid-May through mid-October, crabbers capture their hunt in traps, pull off only the legal-sized claws (at least two and three-fourths inches long), then release the crabs to regenerate the lost appendages, which each can do three to four times in a lifetime. Often only one claw is taken—since one is bigger than the other is—so the crab is not left totally defenseless.

(Stone Crab) Claws and Effect

Even during season, you will not find stone crab claws raw because freezing or even putting the raw claws on ice would cause the meat to stick to the shell before you ever had the chance to cook it. Instead, they are cooked right after their harvest and then either frozen or just kept cold.

Cooking should turn the shells a red-orange and the meat a white tipped with black. (Actually, the meat will look a lot like lobster and sort of tastes like it, too.) If frozen, the shells are supposed to be whole, not broken or cracked.

Because the meat is so rich, you'll only need about three claws per person. A general rule: about two and a half pounds of cooked claws will yield about one pound of meat.

Cooked, but unfrozen, claws can be kept in the refrigerator or packed in ice for as many as two to three days. But it's always wise, and most tasty, to eat them immediately. (Do try our mustard sauce recipe with these.)

If you need to freeze the claws, simply place the claws in an airtight container or bag. Since their shells will protect them, they should be fine for about six months. Thaw in the refrigerator (not out on the counter) for twelve to eighteen hours, not under cold, running water—even though that's fine for most other seafood.

Whether you serve them cold or steamed, don't forget the crackers or a clean mallet or hammer, and lots of napkins. The meat may be difficult to get to, but the prize is certainly worth the work.

If you really want to make an impression, prepare the claws for your guests. Remove the shell and the moveable pincer, but be careful not to break the form of the meat, which is not as easy as it sounds. The meat should come out whole and still attached to the remaining pincer. (And realize you might be serving a cold dinner, which is okay, because we love stone crabs best served cold!)

The Blues

The other important crab in Florida, the blue crab, is also named for its color. But the blue on blue crab is mostly found on its claws. The top of the shell is actually brownish-green; the underside, a creamy white.

Unlike the stone crab, the pincers are not that big, though they still are more than able to hurt you. If they have bright-red tips (consider that a warning sign), it's a female. Another interesting characteristic of both females and males: Each side of the shell draws out to a point.

Blue crabs can live in saltwater or freshwater, as well as in the muddier surroundings of bays, sounds, channels, and river mouths—just about anywhere along Florida's Atlantic and Gulf coasts. Usually, they keep to shallow water, but in the winter, they hibernate in deep water.

Wanted: Dead or Alive

After they're pulled from the sea bottom with everything from dredges to pots and nets, blue crabs come to us year-round live, cooked whole, or as cooked meat (fresh or pasteurized). They average, side to side, five to seven inches.

If live, these crabs should be chilled, not swimming in tanks. Look for movement in the legs or any kind of response when you touch them. Count on about three crabs per person.

If cooked whole, make sure the smell is appealing and the shell a red-orange.

Based on its size and quality, picked meat—which has been cooked—can be categorized (from big to small pieces) as jumbo; lump or backfin; and special, flake, regular, or deluxe. Or it can be sold as claws; cocktail claws that is, a not-so-pretty-but-still-tasty brownish meat. Meat from any other part of the crab should be white. When using crab meat with other ingredients, about one pound is enough for six people.

Until you cook them, live crabs should be kept that way (just one or two days) by putting them in the refrigerator in an open container draped with a damp towel or on ice. Refrigerated below 35° F., fresh, cooked crab and fresh crab meat can last for several days. Sealed pasteurized crab meat, at 32° F., will keep six months.

Blue crab doesn't freeze well in the shell or out of it—or it probably would come that way—so don't try it.

A Clean Break—How To Cook Blue Crab

The dirty work first: Killing live blue crab. It's not so bad, actually. Just drop the crab into boiling water for a minute or so (not too long or you will accidentally cook it). Then run it under cool water to stop the cooking. Now you're ready to steam it or boil it.

Of course, the work's not completely over. You've still got the shell to contend with. To get to the meat, turn the crab upside down and pull back the flap, or apron. Keep pulling down until the top shell comes off. Turn the crab right side up, and remove the gills and any spongy material. Then twist off the claws and legs, and save them for later. Break the body in two. Break the two halves again, so you have four easy-to-deal-with pieces. The rest is fun. Go at it with fingers or a pick, whatever works for you and your friends (a few beers are always good accompaniments). You may need a cracker for the claws and legs.

Though picked crab meat doesn't need much preparation before it can be included in countless dishes—after all, it already has been "picked through" for any shell bits and cartilage—go ahead and look through it again. No one would be more thorough than you, except maybe Martha Stewart (whom we love!).

"Softies"

Like lobster, blue crabs molt. Though it only takes a short time for the blue crab to grow another shell after it sheds its old one in the summer months, it's enough time for a crabber to grab it up. You see, these soft-shell crabs have become a popular dish for Floridians.

Soft-shells are actually caught when they are peelers (blue crabs still with their tough shells but ready to molt) and watched until they discard their old shells. Encased in bodies that are entirely edible (once cleaned) and full of calcium, they are then sold live or frozen. Live soft-shells should be kept chilled and boxed in seaweed or straws. Frozen crabs should be hard as a rock, as if they still were wearing their protective shells. You'll need to pick out at least two per person, that is if you're serving lots of side items, too.

Refrigerated fresh soft-shell crabs will stay alive for a few days and should be used by then. Frozen soft-shell crabs, unlike the hard-shelled blue crabs, will keep very well for up to six months. Thaw them in the refrigerator with a strainer underneath to catch what will turn out to be a lot of extra water.

Before you cook live softies, make sure you clean them. (Frozen soft-shells have already been cleaned.) Use scissors to cut off the eyes and mouth, as well as the spines on the edges of the shell. Turn the crab upside down and cut off the shell's flap, or apron, which can be too chewy. Then lift up each pointed side of the body, and remove the gills. Or you can ask your market to clean them for you.

These are best sautéed, broiled, grilled, or (shamelessly) fried.

The Golden Rules of Golden Crab

The golden crab, a new discovery compared with its Florida cousins, will no doubt be a golden oldie one day because of its delicate flavor. Found on both sides of the state (for the first time in the early 1980s), it is a large, non-swimming crab that averages three to five pounds for a male, smaller for a female.

Trapped in deep water, from five hundred to almost three thousand feet, the golden crab is sold live, refrigerated in cooked halves or clusters, and as chilled, cooked picked meat. Live should mean lively (and should stay that way until cooked); and cooked meat should be white and pleasant to the nose.

Because this is a larger crab, lots of meat will come from the body, claws, and legs, so you won't need as many golden crabs per person as blue crabs.

Refrigerate both fresh and cooked golden crab properly, and fresh crab will keep for a day or two. As was the case with the blue crab, avoid freezing.

To clean golden crab, just follow the rules of the blue crab. But note that the golden shell of this crab will not turn red during cooking like other crabs; it will stay golden. And remember that these legs are much more generous with meat.

Cruise Inn's Crab Dip Appetizer

You can make ahead and let the flavors "marry." Quick and easy for unexpected company, or during a major "crab crave". This recipe is from an old down-home eatery once famous in the tiny town of Palmetto, near Sarasota.

6¹/₂ ounces crab meat, white or special
¹/₂ cup sour cream
1 teaspoon lemon juice
¹/₂ teaspoon Tabasco sauce
¹/₄ teaspoon horseradish
¹/₂ teaspoon salt
Fresh chopped parsley for garnish
Paprika for garnish
White saltine crackers

1. Pick through crab meat very carefully to remove all shell and cartilage.

2. Mix together crab meat, sour cream, lemon juice, Tabasco sauce, horseradish, and salt. Place on crackers, and garnish with parsley and paprika.

SERVES: 6
PREPARATION TIME: 15 MINUTES

CRUISE INN, PALMETTO

Le Petite Fleur's Crab Meat Canapé Lorenzo

This is easy! Use crabs to stuff mushrooms sautéed in wine, or you can spice it up and spread on English muffins with tomato slices topped with Swiss or cheddar cheese.

La Petite Fleur has been closed for more than a decade, but the fond memories of this excellent canapé remain.

8 ounces king crab meat
1 teaspoon butter
2 shallots, minced
1/4 cup chopped green bell pepper
3/4 cup chopped fresh mushrooms
2 tablespoons diced pimiento
1/4 teaspoon English mustard
2 tablespoons Sauterne or other white wine
1/4 cup heavy cream
2 egg yolks, lightly beaten
Salt and pepper to taste
Dash of cayenne
8 trimmed toast squares, cut in quarters
8 slices American cheese, cut in quarters

1. Preheat oven to 300° F.

2. Melt butter in skillet. Sauté shallots, green bell pepper and mushrooms for about 3 minutes. Add pimiento, mustard, and Sauterne. Carefully stir in cream and remove from heat, then stir into egg yolks. Season to taste with salt, pepper, and cayenne.

3. Spread on toast squares and top with cheese. Bake on buttered pan for 5 to 8 minutes or until cheese melts and crab is heated through.

SERVES: 8 TO 10 AS APPETIZER
PREPARATION TIME: 15 MINUTES
COOKING TIME: 15 MINUTES

LE PETITE FLEUR, TAMPA

Derby Lane's Crab Salad à la Grecque

This recipe was given to me by the manager of this once very fancy and very prestigious restaurant at the dog track. The restaurant is more casual now, but this recipe remains only on these written pages.

1 pound fresh lump crab meat
1/4 cup finely chopped onion
2 tablespoons chopped parsley
1 tablespoon chopped pimiento, rinsed and drained
1/4 cup fresh lemon juice, strained
1/2 cup light extra virgin olive oil
1/2 teaspoon oregano
Salt and cracked black pepper to taste.
Olives, radishes, lemon wedges and parsley for garnish

1. Check crab meat for any shells or cartilage and remove; place in mixing bowl. Add onion, parsley, and pimiento. Stir gently and set aside.

2. Make dressing in non-metallic bowl by combining the fresh lemon juice, extra virgin olive oil, and oregano. Add salt and cracked black pepper to taste. Blend well with a wire whisk or in the container of a food processor or blender. Pour over crab meat and toss gently. Refrigerate several hours.

3. To serve, place crab mixture on a plate lined with leaf lettuce. Garnish with black ripe olives, rose radishes, lemon wedges, and parsley.

SERVES: 6 AS A FIRST COURSE, 3 AS A MAIN COURSE
PREPARATION TIME: 10 MINUTES, PLUS TIME TO CHILL

DERBY LANE RESTAURANT, ST. PETERSBURG

Artichoke Felice With Lobster Sauce

Café Chauveron was at one time the most famous restaurant in all of Florida. It was situated on a small waterway a few blocks from Miami Beach and the Atlantic. This recipe from the Café was one of my favorites. Great texture and fabulous flavor!

6 artichoke bottoms, fresh or canned
2 tablespoons butter
1 cup Café Chauveron's Lobster Sauce (see recipe, page 260)
1/2 pound crab meat, picked over
2 tablespoons cognac
1 tablespoon Parmesan cheese

1. Place artichoke bottoms in generously buttered skillet and simmer until warm.

2. In a saucepan, heat lobster sauce. When heated, add crab meat and cognac and boil about 1 minute.

3. Place artichoke bottoms in an oven-proof pan. Stuff with crab mixture, nap* with remaining sauce. Sprinkle with Parmesan cheese and brown under broiler for a few minutes.

* SEE GLOSSARY

SERVES: 3 TO 6 AS FIRST COURSE OR APPETIZER
PREPARATION AND COOKING TIME: 20 MINUTES

CAFÉ CHAUVERON, MIAMI

Captain Bob's Crab Imperial

If you were serving this to guests, we would recommend that you buy whole crab claws. Crab in cans is difficult to pick through to get out all of the shells! This classic is attractive served in small ramekins or seashells. Can be made ahead before a dinner party, refrigerated, and popped into the oven to be served as a first (or main) course.

2 pounds deluxe blue crab meat, or lump crab
2 egg yolks
1 1/2 whole eggs
3/4 cups mayonnaise
1 1/2 teaspoons Worcestershire sauce
2 dashes Tabasco sauce
Pinch thyme
1 teaspoon dry mustard
1 1/2 teaspoons chopped parsley
1 1/2 tablespoons grated Parmesan cheese, optional
Parsley sprigs and paprika for garnish

1. Preheat oven to 450° F.

2. Combine crab meat, egg yolks, whole eggs, mayonnaise, Worcestershire sauce, Tabasco sauce, thyme, dry mustard, chopped parsley, and Parmesan cheese and mix together. Portion into individual serving dishes or place in shallow baking dish. Brush lightly with mayonnaise and sprinkle with Parmesan, if desired.

3. Bake 10 to 15 minutes. Garnish with paprika and parsley.

* SEE GLOSSARY

SERVES: 6 TO 8
PREPARATION TIME: 20 MINUTES
COOKING TIME: 10 TO 15 MINUTES

The Crab Pot, Deerfield Beach

Cruise Inn's Crab Cakes

This delectable recipe makes the lightest crab cakes we have ever tasted. They're nearly all crab, just like Maryland style cakes. Set some of this mixture aside and freeze and use it in Stuffed Perch Oscar (see recipe, page 60).

2 pounds crab meat (1 pound special, 1 pound claw)
2 eggs, well beaten
3/4 teaspoon salt
1/4 teaspoon ground red pepper
1 cup mayonnaise
1/2 cup grated and drained onion
1/4 cup crushed saltine crackers
Tartar sauce or red chili sauce

1. Pick over the crab meat to remove shell or cartilage.

2. Add eggs to a separate glass bowl; add salt and ground red pepper. Beat until pepper has dissolved. Add mayonnaise and drained onion to mixture and blend well. Taste for flavor.

3. Pour over crab meat, add half of cracker crumbs, and stir gently to blend, leaving the crab as whole as possible. The mixture will be rather wet and loose, but it is manageable when cakes are coated with crackers.

4. Shape into 12, 1/2-inch thick, oval or round crab cakes. Dredge them in the remaining cracker crumbs. Press between the hands to make the crumbs adhere and the cakes hold together.

5. Heat oil for deep-frying to 325° F. and deep-fry the cakes in a basket until golden brown all over. Drain and serve hot with tartar sauce or red chili sauce.

SERVES: 4 TO 6 (12 CRAB CAKES)
PREPARATION TIME: 30 MINUTES
COOKING TIME: 20 MINUTES

CRUISE INN, PALMETTO

Captain's Deviled Crab Meat

Here's an excellent and very versatile dish. There are lots of ingredients, but it's easy to prepare. Extra virgin olive oil, sherry, and a good paprika (I love Hungarian!), combine with the crab meat to create a party perfect dish!

1 pound crab meat, fresh or frozen, picked through to remove shell
1 onion, finely chopped
1 stalk celery, finely chopped
1/4 cup finely chopped green bell pepper
1/4 cup finely chopped red pepper
1 clove garlic, finely mashed
1/2 cup extra virgin olive oil or butter
1 tablespoon finely chopped scallions
1/2 teaspoon Worcestershire sauce
1 tablespoon dark prepared mustard
Dash Tabasco sauce
Salt and white pepper to taste
1/4 cup dry sherry
1/4 cup milk
2 whole eggs, lightly beaten
2 tablespoons bread crumbs
Paprika
Chopped fresh parsley, for garnish

1. Sauté onions, celery, peppers, and garlic in extra virgin olive oil or butter until light brown in color. Add crab meat, scallions, Worcestershire sauce, mustard, Tabasco, salt, pepper, sherry, and milk. Bring to boil over low to medium heat.

3. Remove from heat, add eggs and bread crumbs. Mix well.

NOTE: IF USING THIS AS A MAIN DISH, PLACE IN 2-QUART CASSEROLE, TOP WITH PAPRIKA AND PARSLEY, AND BROIL FOR 5 TO 7 MINUTES. IF USING THIS AS AN APPETIZER, SERVE ON TOAST POINTS OR SPOON INTO COQUILLE DISHES AND BROIL FOR 1 TO 2 MINUTES. IF USING AS A STUFFING, PLACE INSIDE FLOUNDER OR OTHER FISH AND BAKE AS USUAL. DO NOT OVERCOOK.

SERVES: 4 AS A MAIN DISH
PREPARATION TIME: 20 MINUTES
COOKING TIME: 10 TO 15 MINUTES

THE CAPTAIN'S TABLE, DEERFIELD BEACH

Dominique's Crab Quiche

Dominique was known for his great French cooking and preparing strange dishes such as kangaroo, white dove, and even bear. This dish is along a more normal vein. Serve for light luncheon or Sunday supper dish with a green salad or tomatoes and basil with vinaigrette.

ONE-CRUST PIE SHELL

1 cup sifted all-purpose flour

1/2 scant teaspoon salt

1/3 cup shortening (half butter or margarine and half shortening, blended together) at room temperature

2 to 3 tablespoons ice water

1. Preheat oven to 425° F.

2. Chill flour in refrigerator for about 5 minutes.

3. Sift flour and salt together. Cut shortening into sifted flour with a pastry blender or your fingertips until the mixture is partially blended. Sprinkle the ice water over the flour mixture, blending lightly with your fingers and adding only enough water to obtain dough that holds together. Roll the dough into a ball and refrigerate wrapped in wax paper for at least 2 hours.

4. Roll dough out to approximately 1/8 inch thick. Place in a creased pie plate or quiche pan, making a rim with your fingers or trimming the edge of the dough to fit the pan. Prick dough all over with a fork and cover with a 14-inch circle of wax paper. Fill with raw rice or uncooked beans to set dough.

5. Bake about 15 minutes. Remove rice or beans and wax paper. Cool.

CONTINUED...

CRAB QUICHE FILLING

3 eggs
3/4 cup light cream
1 cup lump crab meat, well picked over
Partially baked pie shell
1/4 cup grated Swiss cheese
1 pinch each salt and cracked black pepper to taste
2 drops Tabasco sauce
2 tablespoons chives or scallions, chopped

1. Preheat oven to 350° F.

2. Beat eggs. Add cream and blend well.

3. Place crab meat in bottom of pie shell and sprinkle with cheese.

4. Mix together salt, pepper, Tabasco, chives or scallions and add to crab meat.

5. Pour cream and egg mixture over all. Bake 35 to 40 minutes or until knife inserted in middle comes out dry.

6. Cool 10 minutes before serving.

SERVES: 4
PREPARATION TIME: 10 MINUTES FOR SHELL, PLUS 2 HOURS TO CHILL DOUGH; 10 MINUTES FOR QUICHE
COOKING TIME: 15 MINUTES FOR SHELL; 35 TO 40 MINUTES FOR QUICHE

DOMINIQUE'S, MIAMI BEACH, WASHINGTON, D.C.

The Crab Pot's Famous Crab Cakes

These gems are spicy and delicious, and said to be one of the best in the Sunshine State! You can reduce the proportions to suit your fancy, but this recipe is well suited to a party crowd. You can always freeze part and save it for future party hors d'oeuvres.

4 pounds crab meat, shredded
1 pound crab meat, lump
5 eggs
30 crushed saltine crackers
1 cup mayonnaise
5 tablespoons Worcestershire sauce
Fresh chopped parsley
1 cup prepared dark mustard
Salt to taste
1/3 cup all-purpose flour for dredging
Seafood seasoning**
Vegetable oil for frying

1. Preheat oven to 200° F.

2. Pick over crab meat very carefully to remove shells and cartilage.

3. Beat eggs. Using a flat pan, add the 4 pounds shredded crab meat and spread evenly in the pan. Add the crackers, mayonnaise, eggs, Worcestershire sauce, parsley, mustard, salt, and the seafood seasoning. Mix well with your hands. Add the lump crab meat. Shuffle into the mixture gently.

4. Form into 30 cakes and dust with flour. Fry at about 350° F. for about 3 minutes on each side until golden brown. Keep warm in the oven.

** ANY KIND WILL DO, BUT I PREFER OLD BAY® SEASONING

SERVES: 8 TO 10 AS MAIN COURSE
PREPARATION TIME: 20 MINUTES
COOKING TIME: 20 MINUTES

THE CRAB POT, DEERFIELD BEACH

Sea Grill's Crab Norfolk

Michael Wolchik, owner of the Sea Grill, says Crab Norfolk is a recipe originated by his grandfather. You'll enjoy this classic easy favorite of Floridians!

8 tablespoons butter, melted
2 pounds lump crab meat, cartilage removed
Salt and pepper to taste
1/2 cup (4 ounces) dry white wine

1. Place melted butter in a skillet in which the crab is to be served. Add crab meat. Season with salt and black pepper to taste.

2. Sauté over medium-high heat until bubbly and lightly browned. Fluff up carefully without disturbing crab lumps. Turn over and cook again until lightly brown.

3. As you remove skillet from the stove, quickly pour wine (may use less than 1 ounce) around the edges. As it bubbles and sizzles, serve. This is a dish that will not wait.

SERVES: 4
PREPARATION TIME: 10 MINUTES
COOKING TIME: 10 TO 15 MINUTES

SEA GRILL, FORT LAUDERDALE

Alaskan King Crab Legs Dijonaise

This is an easy but elegant dish. Garnish appropriately. You can use almost any crab successfully with this lovely seafood dish.

9 to 12 3-inch pieces king crab legs removed from shell
1 4-ounce jar Dijon mustard
1 cup seasoned bread crumbs
1/4 teaspoon garlic powder
1/4 pound butter
1 cup béarnaise sauce*
1/2 cup fresh whipped cream
Chopped fresh parsley
Parsley sprig

1. Dredge crab legs in mustard. Lightly roll in bread crumbs sprinkled with garlic powder. Sauté in butter until browned. Place in individual baking dishes.

2. Mix béarnaise with whipped cream. Nap* the crab legs.

3. Place under broiler until golden brown. Garnish with chopped parsley and one sprig of parsley.

* SEE GLOSSARY

SERVES: 3 TO 4
PREPARATION TIME: 10 MINUTES
COOKING TIME: 10 MINUTES

THE PLUM ROOM, FORT LAUDERDALE

Key West Crab Cannelloni

The Pier House in Key West makes its own cannelloni shells. You can make your own or purchase them ready-made. I shall never forget my first forkful of this decadently delicious dish!

8 cannelloni shells
1 pound fresh spinach, blanched* and chopped, or may use frozen well-squeezed
1 ounce butter
1/2 cup finely shredded onion
1 clove garlic, finely chopped
2 ounces Pernod**
1/4 pint heavy cream
4 egg yolks
4 ounces crab meat, picked through thoroughly
Salt and pepper to taste
Nutmeg
Homemade tomato sauce, your favorite recipe

1. Prepare cannelloni shells according to package directions. Drain.

2. Squeeze spinach to remove moisture. Set aside.

3. Brown butter in large skillet. Add onion and garlic. Cook until transparent.

4. Add Pernod and flame* dry. Add cream and spinach to mixture. Bring to simmer. Add egg yolks and stir. Add crab meat. Add salt, pepper, and nutmeg.

5. Stuff skins according to package directions. Serve with fresh tomato sauce on top. Be sure it's hot!

* SEE GLOSSARY

** PERNOD IS A YELLOWISH, LICORICE-FLAVORED LIQUEUR SIMILAR TO ABSINTHE. IT IS VERY POPULAR IN FRANCE WHERE IT IS OFTEN SERVED WITH WATER.

PREPARATION TIME: 15 MINUTES
COOKING TIME: 20 MINUTES

THE PIER HOUSE, KEY WEST

Seaport Inn's Soft Shell Crabs Chervil

Try these chervil-kissed crabs for a very aromatic flavored dish. Leaves are curly and dark green and possess an elusive anise flavor that is quite unforgettable. The hollandaise combo brings the crab to a whole new level of gastronomic grandeur.

18 to 24 soft-shell crabs
Salt and pepper to taste
Worcestershire sauce
Flour for dredging
4 eggs
Clarified butter* for frying
2 to 3 shallots, finely chopped
2 to 3 ounces dry white wine
1/2 cup chervil, fresh if possible, or 2 teaspoons dried
Hollandaise sauce*

1. Wash soft-shell crabs gently and very thoroughly. Pat dry. Marinate each in small amount of salt, pepper, and Worcestershire.

2. Lightly dip each crab into flour, then into egg batter. Dip into flour again.

3. Pour clarified butter 1/4-inch deep into heavy iron skillet and heat to about 400° F. This is very hot, so be careful. Place crabs in skillet and cook quickly. Turn once and reduce temperature. Finish cooking slowly. Either place lid on skillet and cook slowly or place in oven and cook slowly for about 5 minutes. Remove crabs and place on serving tray.

4. Remove all but 1 to 2 tablespoons of butter from skillet. To remaining butter add shallots. Fry to a golden brown. Add wine and chervil, reduce heat, and warm through.

5. Mix with hollandaise sauce in a separate bowl. Spread half the sauce mixture over crab and pass the remaining sauce separately.

* SEE GLOSSARY

SERVES: 4
PREPARATION TIME: 15 MINUTES
COOKING TIME: 15 TO 20 MINUTES

SEAPORT INN, NEW PORT RICHEY

The Crab Trap's Crab Crêpes

Your guests will compliment you on this rich, flavorful use for crab of any type.
If you visit The Crab Trap (there are two locations now, in Palmetto and Ellenton),
be sure to try the sautéed turtle!

BATTER

3/4 cup sifted all-purpose flour

1/2 teaspoon salt

2 eggs, beaten

1 cup milk

1 teaspoon melted butter

1. To prepare batter, combine flour, salt, eggs, and milk. Blend until smooth. Add melted butter and blend. Let stand several hours.

2. Heat a 5-inch skillet. Using about 2 tablespoons crêpe batter for crêpe, spread evenly by tilting pan. Brown crêpe on both sides.

3. As each crêpe is done, place in separate pan. Cover to keep warm.

FILLING

2 tablespoons butter

2 tablespoons all-purpose flour

1/2 teaspoon Tabasco sauce

1/4 teaspoon Worcestershire sauce

1/2 teaspoon dry mustard

1/2 teaspoon salt

1 cup evaporated milk

2 tablespoons Parmesan cheese

1 tablespoon cream sherry wine

**3/4 ounces to 1 pound blue crab meat, preferably fresh,
    picked through thoroughly**

Light cream

CONTINUED...

1. Melt butter. Add flour, Tabasco, Worcestershire, mustard, and salt. Blend slowly. Add evaporated milk. Stir until thick.

2. Remove from heat. Stir in Parmesan and cream sherry to make crêpe sauce.

3. Add 1/4 cup of the crêpe sauce to the crab meat and mix.

4. Place 3 tablespoons or 1 1/2 ounces of crab meat mixture into crêpe. Gently roll up. Place rolled crêpe in shallow baking dish. Thin remaining sauce with some light cream and gently spoon over crêpes. Bake at 400° F. for 10 to 12 minutes.

SERVES: 4 TO 6
PREPARATION TIME: 15 MINUTES, PLUS 2 TO 3 HOURS FOR CRÊPES TO SET
COOKING TIME: 15 MINUTES FOR CRÊPES; 20 MINUTES FOR FILLING

THE CRAB TRAP, PALMETTO

La-Te-Da's Soft Shell Crabs With Lemon Ginger Sauce

La Teresita de Marti was named after a famous Cuban leader. Nicknamed "La-te-da", this Key West restaurant no longer sells this dish, but you can prepare it easily in the comfort of your own home. A treat by the pool or in your back yard!

12 small soft-shell crabs
1 1/2 cups plus 1 tablespoon cornstarch
4 tablespoons soy sauce
4 tablespoons sake (Japanese liqueur)
3 eggs
1 tablespoon sesame oil or other vegetable oil
1 cup rice powder, available in Asian food markets
Peanut oil for deep frying
2 teaspoons chopped green chili pepper
1/2 cup coarsely chopped Chinese bok choy
1/2 cup thinly sliced white onions
1/2 cup red peppers in 1/4-inch slices
1/2 cup snow peas
1/4 cup water chestnuts, chopped
1/4 cup bean sprouts
1 teaspoon minced fresh garlic
1 lemon, peeled, reserve rind
1 teaspoon minced fresh ginger
1 1/2 cups chicken stock
1 teaspoon brown sugar
Water

CONTINUED...

1. Clean crabs thoroughly.

2. Mix until smooth: $1/2$ cup cornstarch with 3 tablespoons soy sauce and 3 tablespoons sake. Add eggs and sesame oil.

3. Dip crabs into batter, and then dust them in mixture of 1 cup cornstarch and rice powder. Deep fry at 375° F. in peanut oil in deep skillet until golden brown.

4. Heat peanut oil in wok. As oil gets hot, add chili pepper, bok choy, onions, red peppers, and snow peas. Stir fry until tender but crisp. Add water chestnuts and bean sprouts. Stir together, and then push to side of wok.

5. Prepare mixture of chicken stock, 1 tablespoon of soy sauce, and 1 tablespoon sake. Place garlic, lemon rind, and ginger in oil. Add chicken stock mixture to wok. Add juice from lemon and brown sugar. Mix. Spoon out about $1/2$ cup of this sauce for dip on the side.

6. To thicken sauce in pan, prepare mixture of 1 tablespoon cornstarch and 1 tablespoon water. Add to sauce in wok. If too thick, add chicken stock. Push vegetables back into sauce. Mix with sauce.

7. Place vegetables on serving plates. Arrange crabs on plates. Pour sauce on crabs. Serve dip sauce on side.

SERVES: 4
PREPARATION TIME: 10 MINUTES
COOKING TIME: 10 MINUTES

LA-TE-DA, KEY WEST

NOBODY SHUCKS LIKE ME

Oysters

Ah, Shucks

Throughout history, this bisexual, vegetarian bivalve has been legendary, tirelessly assumed to provide man with great nutrition, food for thought, and the notion—though not necessarily a proven one—of aphrodisiacal powers. Cavemen relished them. The Chinese devoured them as many as two thousand years ago. Cicero ate oysters to nourish his eloquence. The Greeks and Romans wouldn't think of throwing a banquet without dozens of them served on the half shell as a starter. And Louis XI of France insisted that his close group of "great men" of the Sorbonne swallow a certain amount of oysters per day to make them bright.

Though its effects may not be quite as drastic as once believed, the oyster is without question a good source of immunity-boosting minerals such as iron and zinc and is full of vitamin B and magnesium. In fact, oysters are one of the best ways to fill up on iron. Just eat about eight ounces, and you'll have consumed seventy-some percent of the iron requirement for adults.

Like most seafood, oysters also are low in fat, boasting mostly healthy omega-3 fatty acids, and relatively low in cholesterol, lower than once thought. Raw or cooked in a low-fat way, about six medium oysters only carry about sixty calories, two grams of fat, and forty-five milligrams of cholesterol.

Bed Fellows

After it's conceived, a baby oyster, called a spat, will swim along for about two weeks before it settles in. Sticking out its newly grown "foot," it will attach itself for life to a hard object like an old oyster shell, tree branch, or other remnant, something in a brackish area close to the shore where busy currents will provide plenty of food. Inevitably, thousands, maybe millions, of other oysters will also call this bed home.

Here, each can drink as many as twenty-five gallons of water per day while straining food through its gills. How much and what kind of food (mainly single-celled plants) will determine an oyster's flavor and color. Knowing this, it makes sense then that oysters are named after the regions they came from and that their tastes vary.

In the Gulf of Mexico and off the Atlantic coast, we have eastern oysters, a family with many different specific names such as the Apalachicola oysters. Because Florida's estuaries offer warm waters and such a rich environment for oysters, our eastern oysters can reach the market in fewer than two years. Oysters from colder regions, like the Pacific oysters that come from West Coast waters off Northern California and British Columbia, can take as many as six years to reach edible status, but they are not as flavorful.

Open and Shut

Still in their shells, raw oysters need to be alive and chilled on ice when you buy them fresh. Start with those that are closed tight. If any have an opening for someone to peek in (or for something to peek out), tap the shell. As soon as you do, the shell should close in self-defense. If it doesn't and the response instead is a hollow echo, pass it by. (Note that the opposite is true for cooked oysters. If a shell stays closed after it's cooked, it's no good.) The in-shell oyster should be slightly heavy, too, not lightweight.

And don't forget: Your nose knows. With or without shells, raw oysters should be juicy and shouldn't smell offensive, just of the sea.

Fresh shucked oyster meat—when the shell has been removed but the meat is still raw—should be plump and a creamy color. Usually sold in pints, quarts, or gallon containers, the meat should be sitting in no more than ten to fifteen percent liquid. This liquid, or liquor, which came from inside the shell, can be clear, slightly milky, or light gray but shouldn't be pink or have any shell particles or odor to it.

"Selects" are the larger shucked oysters, yielding about thirty per pint; "standards" are average, with about fifty per pint. Beyond these classifications are "large" or "extra select" with about twenty per pint and "small" with sixty or so.

Because some areas, like Apalachicola Bay, harvest oysters year-round, you might be able to find them most of the time. But they may be harder to come by in summer months, since everywhere else in Florida closes the season sometime between June and October.

How Oysters Measure Up

If you're planning on serving oysters in their shells as an appetizer, count on at least a half-dozen per person. As a main meal, you'll need to more than double that.

On the other valve (...I mean, hand), if you're buying shucked oysters, one-fourth to a half-pint per person should do it.

The Cold Facts

Raw oysters will stay alive in their shells about a week if you keep them in the refrigerator, either in a bag with air holes or in an open-top dish covered with a damp cloth or damp paper towel (at 35° to 45° F.). If some shells open up while you're storing them, knock on the shell as you did before. If your resident shuts the door, the oyster's fine. If no one answers, say your good-byes.

Unlike some other seafood, do not seal live oysters in closed containers, and don't place them in water.

Raw shucked oysters will keep for about five days, but they need to stay in containers on ice or in the coldest part of the refrigerator.

If you've opted for frozen raw oysters that are shucked, you will have about two months to decide how to eat them. But make sure they are frozen in airtight containers, and remember to thaw them in those containers either in the refrigerator or under cold, running water. Because freezing oysters will hurt their quality considerably, many times changing flavor, texture, and color, try to reserve thawed oysters for stews or casseroles, or fry them.

Oysters that weren't frozen when you bought them should not be frozen when taken home. You'd be better off giving them away if you can't use them in time.

Raw Deal

Americans love their raw oysters, juice and all, served "on the half shell" (which just means the shell has been torn apart and the empty side abandoned). And that's fine, as long as you know how to keep this bed bug from biting you.

The trick is to stay away from raw oysters during the summer months. Some like to remember this rule by avoiding them during months without an "r" in them: May, June, July, and August. But to be even more safe, you might want to extend that no-eating period from April through the end of September, when the harmful bacterium Vibrio Vulnificus is more prevalent in the Gulf of Mexico and other southeastern regions because of warmer waters.

Besides, the "r" rule also serves as protection for oysters, allowing them recovery time during reproduction months. Some say spawning oysters are less tasty and somewhat watery, anyway.

Some unlucky eaters with certain health conditions, though, are advised to keep their distance from raw oysters all the time. They include anyone with liver disease, hemochromatosis (an iron disorder), diabetes, low stomach acid or a previous stomach surgery, cancer, an immune disorder, or long-term steroid use.

But don't be confused. The bacterium Vibrio Vulnificus is not a pollutant. Though you should always make sure seafood is from a safe area, this bacterium occurs naturally in most seawater. In fact, all seafood has the chance to be contaminated by it. But the key is that most other seafood is cooked before it is eaten, thus killing any danger. So if you're itching for oysters during those hot summer days, help yourself; just cook 'em first.

Shell-Shucked

If you want to serve raw oysters on the half shell, you'll have to do some work first. Of course, with that heavy-duty glove you're supposed to wear, you shouldn't get too dirty. After you rinse and scrub the shell free of mud or grit, place it rounded side down—so as to save most of the liquor—in your gloved hand. Hold the thin end (the bill), and leave the thick part (the hinge) pointing to your other hand.

If it's a large or particularly tough shell, you'll need to hammer the excess lip until you see separation between the two shells. If you're lucky, however, they'll be a gap at the hinged part. Slip your oyster knife, which has a wedge-shaped blade, not a sharp one, into this opening at the base, and pry the shell open by twisting the knife. Then, slide the blade across the top of the shell to cut the muscle.

After you remove the top shell and transfer all its meat to the bottom shell, you can discard it. But don't forget the last step: Slide the blade under any meat still attached to the bottom shell, cutting it free for easy access. Preserve as much of the juice—which should be clear, not pink—as possible.

Bottoms up

You can follow the same steps when you're going to cook oysters without the shell. Obviously, though, you can discard both shells once you've rescued the meat and its liquor. To help you retain all the juice you can, try shucking the oysters over a bowl. Before cooking the meat, too, you'll need to rinse it quickly free of debris and sand.

Cookin' Now

With the hard part out of the way, oysters offer lots of options. Still in their shells, they can be steamed, baked, or roasted; without them, they can be sautéed, fried, or added to soups, stews, and stuffing.

Just don't cook them too long. As soon as the edges start to curl, they're done. And so are you.

Oyster Pot Pie

Good as a luncheon dish or Sunday supper. Serve with salad or cole slaw and a rich dessert.

4 slices bacon, finely chopped
4 tablespoons butter
2/3 cup minced onion
8 drops Tabasco sauce
4 tablespoons lemon juice
1 1/2 pounds oysters, reserve liquor
2 teaspoons salt
1 teaspoon garlic powder
1 teaspoon seafood seasoning
3/4 cup white mushrooms, sliced
1/4 cup Rhine wine
1/2 cup cooked white or brown rice
Baked pie crust top

1. Cook bacon until just crisp. Remove from pan. Pour off most of the fat. Don't wipe the pan out as the small amount of bacon fat helps the flavor.

2. Melt butter in same pan. Sauté onions until just transparent. Add Tabasco and lemon juice.

3. Season oysters with salt, garlic powder, and seafood seasoning. Let oysters come to room temperature before proceeding.

4. Add the mushrooms and wine, and simmer for a few minutes until mushrooms begin to soften. Add bacon and oysters. Cook for 2 to 3 minutes. Don't overcook the oysters.

5. Add cooked rice. Stir carefully and remove from the heat. Cover and keep off the heat for 10 to 15 minutes. If mixture seems to need more moisture, add some of the reserved oyster liquor.

6. Place in 8- to 10-ounce earthenware casserole dish. Place pastry crust on top.

7. Place in hot oven, 450 to 500° F., just long enough to heat through.

SERVES: 4 TO 5
PREPARATION TIME: 15 MINUTES
COOKING TIME: 20 MINUTES

SIPLE'S GARDEN SEAT, CLEARWATER

Selena's Oysters Oreganati

You might try this with the oysters in their half shells. It would look elegant, and as a finger hors d'oeuvre it would be easier to eat. The aroma that this dish sends off transports you right to Italy!

30 oysters, well drained, either canned or fresh shucked
1/2 tablespoon chopped garlic
4 tablespoons bread crumbs
1 tablespoon oregano
1 tablespoon Romano cheese, freshly grated
4 whole canned tomatoes, chopped
Extra virgin olive oil

1. Shuck oysters and drain well. Place shucked oysters in shallow baking dish. Add garlic. Sprinkle with oregano, chopped tomato, bread crumbs, and Romano cheese. Sprinkle with small amount of extra virgin olive oil.

2. Bake until golden brown at 400° F. for about 10 minutes.

SERVES: 5 AS AN APPETIZER OR 2 TO 3 AS A MAIN DISH
PREPARATION TIME: 15 MINUTES WITHOUT HAVING TO SHUCK OYSTERS,
45 MINUTES WITH SHUCKING OYSTERS
COOKING TIME: 10 MINUTES

SELENA'S, TAMPA

Oysters Rockefeller

Serve on rock salt on individual plates, garnished with parsley. Very elegant. Can use this same filling for clams (Clams Rockefeller). One of the best versions of Oysters Rockefeller anywhere!

Rock salt
18 oysters in shells, opened, save liquor
Oyster liquor
1/2 pound fresh spinach, or frozen chopped
1/4 cup butter, softened
1/2 cup finely chopped scallions
1 teaspoon celery salt
3/4 teaspoon garlic salt
1/2 teaspoon white pepper
1/4 teaspoon salt
2 to 3 squirts Tabasco sauce
1 to 2 tablespoons anisette
Bread crumbs, very fine
Parmesan cheese

1. Place enough rock salt in a large baking pan so those half-shelled oysters can rest without tipping. Open oysters, leaving them on the half shell and reserving the liquor. Place oysters on rock salt in baking pan.

2. Wash and chop fresh spinach. Cook in oyster liquor just until wilted. If spinach is frozen, cook in oyster liquor until just defrosted. Drain well and squeeze to remove excess moisture. Process slightly or chop well.

3. Add soft butter and scallions to cooked spinach. Add celery salt, garlic salt, pepper, salt, Tabasco sauce, anisette, and mix well.

4. Add enough very fine bread crumbs to mixture so that stuffing can be molded into small patties, one for each oyster. Place a patty on each oyster and smooth over top.

5. Broil 3 to 4 minutes. Remove from oven. Cover with cheese. Broil again until cheese melts to a light brown. Serve immediately.

SERVES: 3 TO 4
PREPARATION TIME: 1 HOUR, INCLUDING SHUCKING OYSTERS
COOKING TIME: APPROXIMATELY 8 MINUTES

PATE'S, NAPLES

Fresh Oysters With Champagne

You can garnish this dish with caviar to make it extra sumptuous. This dish is particularly delicious when served with the same champagne used in its preparation.

12 fresh oysters
1 shallot, minced
1 cup heavy cream
1/2 cup champagne or sparkling wine
1 tablespoon sweet butter

1. Shuck the oysters, being careful to preserve the juice. Wash the shells and save. The cooked oysters will be served in the original shells.

2. Place the oysters in a saucepan with the oyster juice and cook for 2 to 3 minutes. Remove and keep warm.

3. Add the cream, champagne, and the minced shallot to the hot oyster juice. Cook over a medium heat until the sauce is reduced by one-third. Swirl in the butter. Taste and correct the seasoning if necessary.

4. Serve the oysters in the shells with a bit of the sauce in each one.

SERVES: 2 AS AN APPETIZER
PREPARATION TIME: 15 MINUTES
COOKING TIME: 10 MINUTES

THE DINING GALLERIES AT THE FONTAINEBLEAU HILTON, MIAMI BEACH

Islamorada Oysters Provençale

It is easier to grate the Swiss and mozzarella if they are placed in the freezer for a while.

24 oysters
1 to 2 pounds rock salt
Tomato Concasse (recipe to follow)
¹/₄ pound Parmesan cheese, grated
¹/₄ pound Swiss cheese, grated
¹/₄ pound mozzarella, grated

1. Open the oysters and discard the top shells. Rest the oysters on rock salt spread on flat pan or oven-proof baking dish.

2. Top each oyster with the Tomato Concasse and the cheeses.

3. Place under the broiler until the cheese is browned, no more than 8 minutes.

TOMATO CONCASSE

8 fresh tomatoes, peeled, seeded, and diced
2 scallions or shallots, chopped
Black pepper and Italian seasoning to taste

1. Combine tomatoes and scallions, and bring to a boil. Season to taste.

2. Cool slightly.

SERVES: 4
PREPARATION TIME: 20 MINUTES
COOKING TIME: 15 MINUTES FOR OYSTERS AND CONCASSE

THE CONCH, ISLAMORADA

Oysters Calypso

Diehards may go back to their cocktail sauce, but this is a celebration!
Be sure to loosen the oyster from its shell before dressing.

12 fresh shucked oysters with their half shell
¹/₄ cup sugar
¹/₄ cup hot water
2 ounces fresh ginger root, finely minced
1 bunch fresh coriander, chopped (cilantro or parsley may be substituted)
¹/₂ cup white vinegar
¹/₂ cup fresh pineapple, diced ¹/₈ inch

1. Place fresh oysters on the half shell on crushed ice and refrigerate.

2. Dissolve sugar in hot water. Add ginger root, coriander, and vinegar and mix until well blended.

3. To serve, top each oyster with 1 teaspoon of diced pineapple. Dress liberally with well-blended ginger root and coriander mixture. Serve well chilled.

SERVES: 2
PREPARATION TIME: 15 MINUTES
CHILL

THE PIER HOUSE, KEY WEST

Driftwood's Scalloped Oysters

Years ago I always made a point to dine in this great eatery on the Panhandle. It's been closed for years, but I vividly remember the taste of this luscious oyster casserole. This is a delicious version of scalloped oysters that uses unorthodox ingredients and cooking methods. Serve with crisp bread and a hearty dessert.

5 ounces black ripe olives, cut in large pieces
1 quart oysters
1 cup butter
1/2 cup finely chopped onion
1 teaspoon finely chopped garlic
1 1/2 cups all-purpose flour
1/2 teaspoon paprika
1/2 teaspoon pepper
1/2 teaspoon salt
1 tablespoon Worcestershire sauce
Scant 1/4 cup lemon juice
2 to 3 cups chicken broth
1 cup cracker crumbs

1. Preheat oven to 350° F.

2. Heat oysters in own liquid for 5 minutes. Drain, reserve liquid, and coarsely cut oysters.

3. Melt butter and cook onion and garlic over low heat until tender-crisp. Gradually add flour, stirring constantly until the mixture is golden. Remove from heat and stir in paprika, salt, and pepper.

4. Combine reserved oyster liquid and chicken broth to make 1 1/4 quarts. Add to flour mixture along with Worcestershire and lemon juice. Stir until smooth.

5. Gently stir in oysters and olives and heat through. Pour into casserole dish and top with crumbs. Bake until it just bubbles.

SERVES: 6
PREPARATION TIME: 15 MINUTES
COOKING TIME: 20 MINUTES, DEPENDING UPON HOW LONG IT TAKES TO BUBBLE

THE DRIFTWOOD RESTAURANT, PENSACOLA

Key West Benedict

This is a favorite of the Key West locals. Try it. You'll know why.

Hollandaise sauce*
4 fresh broccoli spears
¼ cup clarified butter*
1 clove garlic, minced
16 fresh oysters
4 English muffins, halved
8 slices Canadian bacon
8 large eggs
1 beefsteak tomato, wedged
Fresh parsley for garnish
2 green manzanilla olives, sliced

1. Prepare hollandaise sauce*, using extra lemon to taste.

2. Poach broccoli spears.

3. Place butter and garlic in sauté pan. Add oysters and sauté until warm.

4. Split muffins and grill. Top with Canadian bacon. Set aside.

5. Poach eggs.

6. Place muffins topped with bacon on serving plate. Place 2 oysters on each piece of bacon. Gently place 1 egg on each muffin and cover with hollandaise sauce. Garnish with broccoli spears and tomato wedges. Sprinkle each serving with parsley and ½ slice of extra virgin olive oil.

* SEE GLOSSARY

SERVES: 4
PREPARATION TIME: 30 MINUTES
COOKING TIME: 20 MINUTES

LA-TE-DA, KEY WEST

Oysters Moscow

This dish is very rich, but the low-fat cream saves a few calories. If you run out of sauce, it takes no time at all to make some more, but you'll have to forego the "marriage". If you have any leftover sauce, use as a dressing over chopped lettuce.

24 fresh whole oysters
¹/₄ cup white horseradish
¹/₄ cup low-fat sour cream
¹/₄ cup buttermilk
1 ounce caviar

1. Open the oysters and discard the top shells.

2. Combine horseradish, sour cream, and buttermilk. Blend well. Refrigerate sauce for a few hours to allow flavors to meld.

3. Top each oyster with a little caviar and sauce.

SERVES: 4
PREPARATION TIME: 1 MINUTE, PLUS "MELDING" TIME

THE CONCH, ISLAMORADA

STEAMED CLAM

Clams

Value Meal

Europeans don't feel quite the same about clams as we do. In this case, they more or less think the American Indians unduly influenced the eating habits of the early colonists. You see, the Indians were avid clam eaters, and, luckily for us, they shared their love of clams, showing the colonists how to gather, cook, and eat them.

But the taste of clams wasn't their only value to the Indians. The Indians were so impressed with the purple interiors of some clams that they used the interiors as their most important currency.

Though we never took the fascination that far, Americans certainly have carried on the tradition of enjoying this sweet seafood treat, once again to the delight of nutritionists.

Just one serving of clams offers two days' worth of iron and a forty-day supply of vitamin B. Considering clams are also low in fat and cholesterol and high in protein, calcium, potassium, zinc, and vitamins A and C, it seems the Indians, in a way, did strike gold.

The Hogs vs. the Squirts

There are many, many varieties of clams, some hard-shell clams, others the soft-shell type.

You've come to know the hard-shell clam, because that is what we usually see in Florida markets and restaurants. The northern quahog and the southern quahog are the most important commercially here. Harvested year-round from sandy bays and along the beaches of central and east coast Florida, they are nearly oval and have thick, brown shells. (Other hard-shell clams come from our deeper waters or from the Pacific and can vary from white to gray to brown.)

You can read the rings on the quahog's shell much as you would read the wrinkles on a human's face, both signs of age. The quahog can live about thirty years and grow to be as many as four and a half inches wide, though two and a half inches is more standard. As do other hard-shell clams, it uses a foot to bury itself in the sand and a neck, or siphon, to filter seawater and food through its body.

Soft-shell clams, also found in both oceans, are not like soft-shell crabs, which you're probably more familiar with. You cannot eat the shell of soft-shell clams; they're just so-named because they are less brittle than their harder-shelled cousins.

Also called a steamer, gaper, and squirt—to name a few—the soft-shell clam has a neck, too, but this one protrudes from the shell, preventing it from closing completely. They're usually stark white, even though they come from muddier areas.

Small, medium, and large (in other words) quahog clams are named and sold according to their sizes. Chowder is the biggest at about two and a half inches or more. You'll only get one to two of these per pound. Cherrystone grows to about two inches; top neck, one and a half; middle neck, one and one-fourth; and little neck, one inch. About ten to thirteen little necks will come per pound.

Keep in mind: the bigger, the more meat but the less tender. So save the real "hogs" for soups and stews and such.

All Tapped Out?

You can buy quahog clams live in the shell, already shucked, or canned. (Clam broth, juice, and nectar are also sold bottled or canned.)

There's no surprise that the best way to get them is live. Live clams should not be kept directly on ice or in water or stored in airtight containers. Any of these will kill them.

How do you know which already have "kicked the bucket" and which haven't? Easy. Just look for the Do Not Disturb sign. Well, not literally. But that's what the clam is telling you when it has its shell shut tight: "I'm alive but do not want to be bothered."

Before you discard any clams that are slightly open, tap each, and see if you get a reaction. If any do not close, do not buy them. Discard any with broken shells, too.

Feel the weight of the shells, if possible. If they're too heavy, they are probably filled with sand; if too light, they're probably dead. And use your nose. That hard-to-forget stench of dead shellfish will tell you all there is to know.

Shucked clams should be plump, sweet smelling, and sold in airtight containers. They should be sitting in their own liquor, a clear or opalescent liquid that has no shell bits floating about.

You'll need about six to ten of the average-sized clams per person. If shucked, that means about one quart for six people.

Staying Power

Live clams will stay alive for up to a week if you'll keep them refrigerated in a container with the top at least partly off. Try covering them, loosely, with a damp towel so they don't dry out. Remember to drain the liquid daily, too.

Shucked clams need to be in airtight container and can be kept only for about five days.

If dinner plans change for the week, you can freeze live clams (not shucked clams). Just place them in a heavy freezer bag and seal it after releasing any air. You'll have about three months.

To make it even easier, you won't even need to thaw the clams. Just go on with the recipe.

Comin' Clean

Fresh quahog clams can be very sandy, to say the least. To clean them, first scrub their shells with a brush, rinse them, then soak them in cold brine (one-third cup salt to each gallon of water). Throw away any that float. Do not keep them in the water for more than twenty minutes or so, though, or you'll kill them. Sprinkle one-fourth cup cornmeal on the top for each quart of clams, and let them sit (refrigerated) for three to twelve hours. It will whiten them and rid them of the sand and black material in their stomachs. Then rinse them off again.

This is especially important if you're going to eat them raw. Of course, the real trick is still ahead.

An Inside Job

To get to the jewels, you'll have to sacrifice some time and a little sweat. It's worth the risk, and trouble, if you know how to shuck quahogs properly.

Hold the clam in the palm of your hand with its hinge near your thumb. Slip a paring or clam knife between the two shells at the rounded edge. Wiggle it around until you separate the shells, but try not to push the knife too deep while doing so. Otherwise, you'll chop the meat into pieces. Then cut the meat from the top shell and transfer it into the bottom shell. Save as much of the liquor as possible. Detach the meat from the bottom shell and remove (unless you're serving it raw in the shell).

A few helpful tips: If your clam is playing tough, and you just can't wedge your knife between the two shells, try spinning it in your hand or on the counter. Eventually, the clam will give. If that's not your style, stick any hard-nosed clams in the freezer for a few minutes or more, just until they lose the will to "clam shut."

Also, since you'll want to save as much of the clam juice as possible, shuck your clams over a bowl. Just realize you'll have shell pieces and other undesirables you'll need to pick out.

Of course, you could have your fish dealer clean and shuck the clams for you, but only if you're going to cook them (out of their shells) right away and obviously not if you are serving them raw on the half shell. Keep in mind, too, that you'll want to remind them to keep the liquor.

Over Easy

No matter which size of quahogs you're cooking what way, don't overcook them. They should be soft and juicy. In fact, they are sometimes eaten raw on the half shell, so they obviously don't need much cooking time to taste good. Otherwise, you'll be giving your mouth a not-so-appreciated workout since they tend to get tough and rubbery when overdone.

One way to know when to ring the dinner bell is to watch the shells open as you cook them. As soon as they do, the meat should be done. Throw away any clams that do not open.

Of the quahogs, littlenecks through cherrystones can be eaten raw or baked, sautéed, steamed, or fried. Because they are bigger and tougher, the chowders are great either stuffed or chopped up for (take a wild guess) chowders and fritters.

Steamed Clams

Cap's Clams Casino

This is incredible; so good, in fact, you may be an instant winner at the casino. Have the fishmonger open the clams for you if you don't know how.

4 pounds fresh, hand-shucked clams, about 60 to 80 half-shell clams, depending on size, chopped or ground up, shells reserved

1 pound butter

$^1/_4$ cup Worcestershire sauce

$^1/_4$ cup chopped parsley

4 cups finely chopped green bell peppers

2 cups finely chopped red onions

1 teaspoon mace

$^1/_8$ cup seafood seasoning

6 whole eggs

$^1/_4$ cup lemon juice

1 tube anchovy paste

1 to 2 cups bread crumbs

Bacon strips on top

1. Grind or mince clams in blender.

2. Mix all other ingredients in a separate bowl.

3. With a tablespoon, scoop one spoon clams per half clamshell. Place a spoon of batter dressing and a small strip of bacon on top of the clam.

4. Broil on middle rack until browned, heated through to bottom of clams

SERVES: 8 TO 10
PREPARATION TIME: SHUCKING TAKES A LONG TIME, PLUS 20 MINUTES
COOKING TIME: 5 MINUTES

CAP'S SEAFOOD RESTAURANT, ST. AUGUSTINE

Joyce's Garlic Clam Dip

Great flavorful dip with lots of juicy clams! Shallots and chives make the difference.

1 6½-ounce can chopped clams
2 tablespoons clam broth, reserved from clams
1 8-ounce package cream cheese, softened (Use low-fat if watching calories)
½ tablespoon finely chopped shallots
1 tablespoon Worcestershire sauce
1 teaspoon chopped chives, dried or fresh
1 teaspoon Beau Monde seasoning
1 clove garlic, minced
1 bunch chives for garnish

1. Drain clams, reserving clam juice.

2. Combine cream cheese and clam juice in separate bowl.

3. Mix the remaining ingredients together. Beat into cream cheese mixture. Add clams.

4. Chill and garnish with chives. Serve with crackers or fresh vegetable dippers.

SERVES: 6 TO 8
PREPARATION TIME: 10 MINUTES
CHILL

JOYCE LAFRAY'S HOME, ST. PETERSBURG

Steamed Clams, Minorcan Style

The Ponce family, who claim to be direct descendants of Ponce de Leon, sent the message, "You'll enjoy this old Minorcan specialty; our customers do!" They're right. It's great. Have a couple dozen.

1 dozen fresh clams, in shell
2 ounces butter
4 onions, sliced ¼-inch thick
2 ounces Worcestershire sauce
2 stalks celery, cut in half
Fresh whole black peppercorns

1. Combine all ingredients in a large kettle with shallow layer of salted water. Be sure that the clams have been cleaned well.

2. Cover and steam for 8 to 10 minutes or until all the clams are opened. Discard any that haven't opened.

3. Place steamed clams in a shallow dish and pour broth over them.

SERVES: 1
PREPARATION TIME: 5 MINUTES
COOKING TIME: 8 TO 10 MINUTES

CAPT. JIM'S CONCH HUT, ST. AUGUSTINE

Clams With White Sauce

My friend Chef Salvatore Ponzo, who was head chef at this now-closed eatery, suggests two leaves of fresh basil be added to the sauce for more zip. Chef also suggests that you reserve six clams, steam them open separately, then add them—in their shells—to the dish at the very last minute. You're gonna love it!

If you would prefer a red sauce, follow this recipe but instead of broth, add two cups of your favorite marinara sauce.

18 fresh littleneck clams, shucked and coarsely chopped
Italian parsley, chopped, to taste
4 garlic cloves, peeled and crushed
1 pinch white pepper
1 anchovy fillet in extra virgin olive oil, finely chopped
1/4 cup extra virgin olive oil
1 pinch granulated garlic powder
1 cup very light broth, chicken or diluted clam juice, warmed
1/2 pound linguine, cooked al dente*

1. Add oil to skillet and bring almost to a sizzling point. Add the chopped garlic, anchovy, and parsley, and cook until brown.

2. Add the chopped clams. Simmer for about 5 minutes.

3. Add the white pepper, the granulated garlic powder, and the warmed broth. Let cook for a few moments, just until flavors are mixed. Taste for seasoning.

4. Serve over linguine.

* SEE GLOSSARY

SERVES: 2
PREPARATION TIME: 15 MINUTES
COOKING TIME: 8 TO 10 MINUTES

THE SEAPORT CHEF, ST. PETERSBURG

Sweet Mouth Bass

WALLOP SCALLOP

Scallops

Sweet Treat

Scallops have given us more than great nutrition. The beautiful shape of their fan-shaped shells has decorated everything from writing paper to gas stations. The shell itself is a work of art, thin and incredibly strong, with fluting that radiates a fan from the hinge to the edge of the shell. Shells come in a myriad of colors, from white to black, in yellows, tans, reds, purples, and steely blues.

Scallops are the origin of the cooking term "scalloped," which originally meant seafood that was creamed, heated, and served in a scallop shell. Now "scalloped" ranges from a form of potato casserole to the decorative edge of a pie crust.

In medieval times, the shells were carried by pilgrims as evidence of their visit to the Galician shrine of Santiago de Compostella, to pray before the body of St. James. The pilgrims were required to eat the mollusks as penance, and on the return trip they wore the shells as a badge on their hats.

These days, eating the meat is rarely an act of penance. More often, it's a delight to sample the meat from these bivalves. They have high levels of well-balanced protein, very little fat, and many essential minerals and vitamins. And they contain about twenty calories an ounce.

Scallops can be cooked in so many ways: scalloped, fried, broiled, sautéed, or used in cocktails, stuffings, soups, and salads. They can be used in almost any recipe for fish salads or creamed fish.

On the Move

Scallops are the liveliest of all the bivalve mollusks. Unlike their oyster cousins, they are jet-propelled swimmers. As they flap their shells open and closed, they shoot strong jets of water from the two sides of the shell hinge, so they soar like a rocket. On a clear day you can see them in tide pools skipping about, snapping their shells in great glee. When captured, they beat their valves wildly in an attempt to escape, sounding like clacking false teeth.

Credit the scallop's single adductor muscle with opening and closing the shell. This powerful muscle, larger than in other mollusks, provides us with the lean, light, firm meat with such a delicate, sweet flavor.

Wet and Wily

While they're lively in the water, scallops die as soon as they're removed from the water. You'll rarely see them in your market in their shell. Commercial fishermen shuck them immediately at sea and ice them for your local store.

You can also catch your own. Florida produces two kinds of scallops: the bay scallop and the calico, both about the same size. The best hunting grounds are the eelgrass in shallow waters. Grab a mask and fins, attach a sack to your waist, and you can pluck them from the grass or snag them as they swim by. Before you don a snorkel, though, check with the Marine Patrol about licenses, limits, and seasons. When you take them out of the water, you can eat them raw or cooked right away. They die quickly once they're on dry land.

At home, scrub them thoroughly. You can put them in a 300° F. oven, deep shell down, until they open. Or insert a knife between the shells near the base of the scallop. Toss away the top shell and the dark mass that surrounds the white muscle. Then you can carve that adductor right out.

It's best to use scallops the same day you bought them, but they will keep in the refrigerator for a day or two. If it will be awhile, freeze them raw. (Cooked scallops that are frozen lose their moisture, texture, and flavor.) Wash them well and pack them tightly together in an airtight, moisture-proof container. Thaw them in the refrigerator or under cold running water. Raw, frozen scallops will keep for three to four months in the freezer.

Tiny Treasures

Bay and calico scallops are very tiny, with a muscle about 1/2 inch in diameter. The meat will be sweet and moist when cooked. While you're shopping, make sure they have a mild, slightly sweet, odor and are free of liquid. Sea scallops are larger (about 1 1/2 inches in diameter), but are not as tender. They are perfect for salads and creamed dishes. After cooking, slice them in thirds against the grain.

The color of scallops ranges from pale beige to creamy pink. If they are pure white, walk away. They're probably been soaked in water to increase their weight.

Allow a third of a pound of sea scallops or a quarter-pound of bay scallops per serving for sautéing or broiling.

Quick and Easy

Never overcook scallops if you want to retain their natural tenderness, succulence, and flavor. Bay and calico scallops should be poached only two minutes, sautéed one to two minutes, or baked five to eight minutes. Sea scallops should be poached only four minutes, sautéed two to three minutes, or baked five to eight minutes.

Miami Beach Spicy Ceviche

Try this as a tantalizing first course. Fillet of sole, cut in $1/3$-inch cubes, is a good substitute.

1 pound scallops—if sea scallops, cut into $1/3$-inch cubes
$1/2$ cup extra virgin olive oil
$1/2$ cup vegetable oil
$1/4$ cup fresh coriander leaves or 2 teaspoons cracked coriander seeds
$1/2$ cup black olives
$1 1/2$ cups minced Spanish onions
$2/3$ cup lime juice
3 cloves garlic, minced
2 crushed bay leaves
Freshly ground black pepper to taste
1 pinch of salt
3 drops Tabasco sauce
$1/2$ cup finely chopped celery
$1/2$ cup finely chopped fresh scallions

1. Place scallops or cubed fish in a shallow glass bowl.

2. Blend extra virgin olive oil, vegetable oil, and coriander leaves. If using coriander seeds, cook seeds in a portion of the oil for 5 minutes and add to the remaining oil.

3. Combine oil mixture with olives, onions, lime juice, garlic, and crushed bay leaves.

4. Pour marinade over fish. Sprinkle with pepper and salt. Add Tabasco and chopped celery. Cover bowl and chill fish for 24 hours.

5. Serve cold on a bed of lettuce with some of the marinade. Sprinkle with fresh scallions.

SERVES: 8 APPETIZERS
PREPARATION TIME: 10 MINUTES
CHILL: 24 HOURS

DOMINIQUE'S, MIAMI BEACH, WASHINGTON, D.C.

Scallops Singapore

This can be served as an appetizer or a main course, as it is easy to double or triple the recipe. Substitute soy sauce if oyster sauce is not available.

2 tablespoons peanut oil
1/4 teaspoon salt
10 ounces bay scallops
1 inch sliced ginger, peeled, smashed, and chopped
8 large mushrooms, sliced in thirds
1/2 tablespoon sherry
1/2 cup chicken broth
1 scallion, trimmed and shredded
1 tablespoon Asian oyster sauce, available in groceries or import food stores
1 tablespoons cornstarch.

1. Heat peanut oil in a wok or large skillet over medium high heat. Add salt. Add scallops and ginger and stir briefly. Add mushrooms and sherry.

2. Stir constantly while adding chicken broth, oyster sauce, and scallion. Stir and gradually add cornstarch until sauce starts to thicken. Serve immediately.

SERVES: 2
PREPARATION TIME: 10 MINUTES
COOKING TIME: 10 MINUTES'

MAI-KAI, FORT LAUDERDALE

Raimondo's Artichokes Julann With Scallops

This is an extremely attractive dish to serve. The color combination of the artichoke, caviar, and sauces creates a dramatic first course.

ARTICHOKES

4 small artichokes
1 cup dry white wine
Juice of 2 lemons
Water

1. Place artichokes in a large pot with the wine and lemon juice. Add enough water to cover the artichokes. Cover and blanch* until done, about 30 minutes. Remove artichokes and cool.

2. Cut out the centers of the artichokes. They will be stuffed later with the scallops.

SCALLOPS

12 ounces of bay scallops
1 cup champagne
2 shallots, finely chopped
Touch of cayenne pepper
Pinch of salt

1. Wash the scallops well and dry. Blanch* them in a combination of champagne, shallots, cayenne pepper, and salt. Before they are completely cooked, remove and let cool.

2. Reduce* the champagne mixture to an essence, about a tablespoon. Let cool.

* SEE GLOSSARY

CONTINUED...

S A U C E

1 teaspoon dry English mustard
Juice of 1 lemon
2 egg yolks
1 cup very fine extra virgin olive oil
2 whole pimientos, puréed in blender or food processor
Beluga caviar
Chopped parsley
Champagne or wine

1. Remove the champagne essence from above and place into a mixing bowl. Add mustard, lemon juice, and the egg yolks and whisk together.

2. Add the extra virgin olive oil, a few drops at a time, mixing constantly, keeping the mixture thick and smooth. Use the same procedure as for making mayonnaise. Add and stir in the pimientos.

3. Fold the scallops into the sauce carefully. Fill the artichoke centers with the sauced scallops. Top with caviar.

4. To the remaining sauce, add enough chopped parsley to color it green. Thin with a little wine or champagne so that it will nap* easily.

5. To serve, turn outside leaves of the artichoke down and pour the green sauce around the artichoke, over the turned-down leaves.

* SEE GLOSSARY

SERVES: 4 AS AN APPETIZER
PREPARATION TIME: 30 TO 45 MINUTES
COOKING TIME: 45 MINUTES

RAIMONDO'S, CORAL GABLES

Scallop Terrine

Easy recipe...great results. Chef Tom Klauber's original. You must try it!

1 ¹/₂ pounds fresh baby bay scallops
3 cups heavy whipping cream
6 whole eggs
¹/₄ pound fresh clean spinach
¹/₂ teaspoon saffron
1 cup dry white wine
Salt and pepper

1. Warm 1 cup heavy cream and stir in saffron until mixture is bright yellow. Let cool.

2. In the container of a food processor, mix until smooth: ¹/₂ pound scallops, 2 eggs, 1 cup heavy cream, ¹/₃ cup dry white wine, salt, and pepper. Remove and set aside in refrigerator.

3. Clean bowl for processor and mix until smooth: ¹/₂ pound scallops, 2 eggs, saffron-cream infusion, ¹/₃ cup dry white wine, salt, and pepper. Remove from bowl and refrigerate.

4. In a terrine, layer as follows: white/green/yellow/green/white. Bake in water bath at 350° F. for 1 hour. Let cool overnight.

SERVES: 4 TO 6
PREPARATION TIME: 20 MINUTES
COOKING TIME: 1 HOUR
CHILL: OVERNIGHT

THE COLONY RESTAURANT, LONGBOAT KEY

Scallops Mousseline

This recipe was given to me by the owners of Andrew's Second Act, a popular eatery in Tallahassee. The core group of politicos hangs out here. It's easy to guess why.

Use a good hollandaise sauce in this recipe, as it is a dominant, but not overpowering, part of the recipe. If you have extra hollandaise, freeze it in dollops. Heat over a double boiler, whisking all the time before using it in a recipe. This dish is perfect for luncheon, a light supper, or as an elegant appetizer.

2 pounds bay or sea scallops
2 tablespoons butter
Salt and pepper
2 teaspoons lemon juice
2 tablespoons heavy cream, whipped
3 to 4 tablespoons hollandaise sauce*

1. Sauté the scallops in 2 tablespoons butter. Use an oven-proof pan. When almost done, add salt, pepper, and lemon juice.

2. Fold the whipped cream into the hollandaise and spread over the scallops. Place under the broiler until golden.

* SEE GLOSSARY

SERVES: 4 TO 6
PREPARATION TIME: 10 MINUTES
COOKING TIME: 5 MINUTES

ANDREW'S SECOND ACT, TALLAHASSEE

Scallops in Green Sauce

The remaining sauce is delicious served over pasta.

1¹/₂ pounds scallops
2 cups sliced mushrooms
1 cup dry white wine
1¹/₂ teaspoons salt
1 cup watercress leaves
2 cups spinach leaves
(4 ounces greens in all)

1. Place scallops, mushrooms, wine, and salt in saucepan over medium heat until it almost comes to a boil. Scallops will whiten but barely cook through. Stir occasionally. Strain liquid into another pot. Cover scallops to prevent drying out.

2. Add greens to liquid in the pan, stir and bring to a boil. Greens should be just wilted. Remove with a slotted spoon into the container of a food processor or food mill. Purée.

3. Reduce* liquid to ¹/₂ cup and place into the container of a food processor with greens. Blend until smooth.

SAUCE FOR SCALLOPS

2 egg yolks
2 tablespoons cream
¹/₄ teaspoon white pepper
1 cup vegetable oil or ¹/₂ extra virgin olive oil, ¹/₂ peanut oil

1. Add yolks, cream, and white pepper to greens in processor. Gradually add oil and process.

2. Serve scallops in shells with sauce.

* SEE GLOSSARY

SERVES: 4 AS APPETIZER
PREPARATION TIME: 15 MINUTES
COOKING TIME: 15 TO 20 MINUTES;
DEPENDS ON HOW LONG IT TAKES TO REDUCE JUICES

SWANSON'S BISTRO AND WINE BAR, CLEARWATER

Lauro's Fresh Sea Scallops

Tasty and simple to prepare. You might serve it over rice or pasta.

1 pound fresh scallops
Seasoned all-purpose flour
¹/₄ cup extra virgin olive oil
1 clove garlic, crushed
Pinch of salt
Pinch of crushed red pepper
¹/₄ cup dry white wine, or to taste
6 ounces peeled plum tomatoes, chopped

1.   Wash the scallops. Drain and pat dry. Dip in the seasoned flour (salt, pepper).

2.   Pour the extra virgin olive oil into a frying pan and heat. When the oil is very hot, add the scallops and the garlic. When the scallops are golden brown, add the salt, red pepper, wine, and tomatoes.

3.   Simmer for 4 to 5 minutes. Taste for seasoning.

SERVES: 2
PREPARATION TIME: 10 MINUTES
COOKING TIME: 4 TO 5 MINUTES

LAURO'S RISTORANTE, TAMPA

Startled Scallops

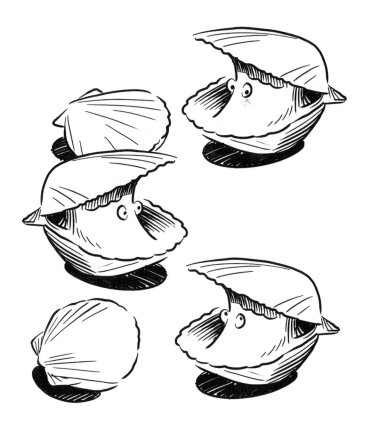

MUSSEL MAN

Mussels

Dinner Mystery

Mussels probably are one of the greatest unused resources in the United States. Yet in Europe demand is so great that mussels have been propagated to augment the natural supply. The history of mussels in Europe dates back to prehistoric times. Mussel shells fill European middens found along the Atlantic coast, but the shells are few and far between on this side of the pond. Legend has it that once the mussel eaters arrived on these shores, Native Americans told them the mussels here were poisonous, and the newcomers took their word for it.

There's some truth to the rumor. Mussels are susceptible to water pollution. Like other bivalves, they continuously strain water and the toxins in it, passing what they catch along to those who eat them.

Mussels that are propagated are done so under suitably strict conditions. They are plump, delicious, and safe.

Versatility Plus

There are dozens of mussel species, but the most abundant variety is the blue or common mussel. This delicate bivalve has a thin, blue-black shell, measuring two to three inches long, with a deep violet color inside. Other species range from one and a half to six inches, and can be indigo blue to bright green to yellowish-brown. In days gone by, freshwater mussels were exploited for the mother-of-pearl inside the shell rather than the meat.

Mussels are found in all the world's oceans. They spin a very strong, silken black thread called "byssus" or "beard" to anchor themselves to underwater objects. The best-tasting are harvested from colder waters. The creamy-tan meat is slightly sweet, but a little tougher than clams or oysters.

No mussels are taken commercially in Florida. They generally are too small and too few to make it worthwhile. Fresh mussels sold here generally are shipped from Puget Sound or New England. Because mussel culture requires less time and effort than oysters, they usually are cheaper than their bivalve cousin.

There are limitless ways to prepare mussels: broiled, fried, simmered, scalloped, added to soups or omelets, smoked, curried, marinière, as fritters, as a stuffing, with spaghetti, stewed, in a bouillabaisse, or as a garnish to fish dishes. They can be steamed, removed from their shells, breaded, and served much like oysters or clams. Or they can be served with a sauce, shell and all. Mussels can be used in just about any dish that calls for clams or oysters. Don't throw away the shells. They make beautiful serving dishes.

Eat 'em Fast

Mussels can be purchased in the shell alive or canned in either brine (a hot barbecue sauce) or smoked. The shells of the fresh live ones should be tightly closed. If there is a gap between the shells, knock on the door. A good mussel will snap shut. Avoid those with broken shells or ones that feel light and loose when shaken. That means the mussel is probably dead. Be on the lookout for "mudders," mussels filled with mud rather than meat. To check, try to slide the two halves of the shell across each other. If they budge, you've hit mud.

Mussels are very perishable, so you should cook and eat them the same day you buy them. Get about five pounds of live ones for six servings, or one to two dozen per person for a main dish.

Good Housekeeping

Once they're in the kitchen, clean them under cold running water, scrubbing with a stiff brush to remove the mud and the "beard" that protrudes on the edges. Place them in a pot, cover them with cold water, and let stand for two hours. Live mussels will drop to the bottom. Dead ones will float to the surface. Discard the dead mussels.

To open, place a pan on the table to catch the liquid that you'll want to save for sauce. Hold the clean mussel over the pan. Insert a knife between the shells in the bearded area and run a blade around the edge, working first toward the beard end. Remove the meat, trim away any remaining whiskers, and place the meat in a separate dish from the liquid. Strain the liquid through two layers of cheesecloth to remove any sand or shells.

Heat and Eat

Mussels cook very quickly. They are done just as soon as they have opened their shells.

To steam, put one inch of water into a pot. Add salt and bring to a boil. Slide cleaned, unshelled mussels gently into the pot. cover and simmer three minutes or less—just until they open. Remove mussels carefully; don't lose the liquid inside the shells if you want sauce. Once they're cool enough to handle, pour the liquid through cheesecloth. Remove the shell, trim the whiskers, and taste for doneness. If they are not quite done, you can place them back in the pot for one to three minutes.

Raintree's Moules Marinière

The chef says you can adjust the seasonings to your own taste. Serve this dish with lots of crusty French bread to soak up the delicious sauce. This is a classic dish in France and Belgium, where nearly every restaurant worth its salt has it on the menu!

24 to 48 mussels, depending on size and appetite
1/2 cup unsalted butter
1 1/2 to 2 onions, finely chopped
Basil to taste
Marjoram to taste
4 cloves garlic, minced
2 cups dry white wine
1 cup heavy cream

1. Scrub the mussels and remove the beards. Discard any that are already open.

2. In a large, heavy-based pan, melt the butter. Add the onions, herbs, and garlic, and cook over medium heat until the onions are translucent. Add the mussels to the pan. Cover tightly and turn the heat up.

3. Shake the pan during the cooking process so that all the mussels get equal heat and don't stick. Cook just until all the mussels are open (check in about 30 seconds).

4. Remove the lid and pour in the wine and the cream. Reduce the heat and cook for 2 to 3 minutes, shaking the pan gently so that the sauce is mixed with the mussels.

5. To serve, ladle the mussels and sauce into four individual serving bowls. Or you may serve them "family style" from one large serving dish, letting everyone take their mussels from the community dish. Have a separate dish for the shells.

SERVES: 4
PREPARATION TIME: 30 MINUTES, INCLUDING CLEANING OF MUSSELS
COOKING TIME: 15 MINUTES

RAINTREE RESTAURANT, ST. AUGUSTINE

Mussels in Cream Sauce

If you're a mussel lover, or even if you're not, you'll enjoy this. Serve steaming hot!

4 pounds fresh mussels, well-cleaned and scrubbed to remove all sand
2 cups water
2 cups dry white wine
Juice of 1 lemon
2 shallots, chopped
¹/₄ pound butter
1 cup all-purpose flour
3 egg yolks
8 ounces heavy cream
Salt and pepper to taste
1 bunch parsley, chopped

1. Place the mussels in a large pot with water, wine, and lemon juice. Steam 7 to 8 minutes or until shells open. Reserve liquid.

2. Place each mussel on shell half. Arrange on large heatproof platter or individual plates.

3. Strain liquid through a cloth napkin.

4. Sauté shallots in butter. Add flour, stirring constantly with a whisk until smooth. Add reserved liquid. Stir until medium thick. Beat in egg yolks, cream, and parsley, stirring. Taste for seasoning.

5. Anoint the mussels with sauce and serve hot.

SERVES: 4 AS ENTRÉE, 8 AS APPETIZER
PREPARATION TIME: 20 TO 30 MINUTES
COOKING TIME: 8 TO 10 MINUTES

PETITE MARMITE, PALM BEACH

Mussel Men

KING CONCH

Conch

Key West Conch—Big and Beautiful!

Just about anyone who has walked along the beaches of Florida has found those beautiful, spiral-shaped, spiky shellfish called conch (pronounced "conk"). They are particularly abundant in the Key West area. In fact, Key West residents themselves are often referred to as conchs.

The shells have been used for decorations, to "listen to the ocean," and as horns. They even have been ground up to make porcelain and burned to make lime. On occasion, pearls have been found in the Queen Conch, which is native to the Bahamas.

Greet and Meat

Shallow water, coral reefs, and rocks are good places to hunt for conch. To see whether a conch is alive, tap the "trapdoor." If it closes, the conch is alive. Check with the locals on limits and the right time of season to gather them.

These snails drag themselves around with their single, muscular foot—the edible part of the conch. If you buy them fresh in their shells, make sure the shell is shiny and the meat is firm and clean looking. Conch should smell fresh and of the sea.

To remove the meat from the conch, knock the bulging side with a hammer to help break the shell. Insert a knife and twist it around until you feel the muscle being severed. Grab whatever is sticking out and pull hard. Then cut away the stomach and tail, and peel off the tough, leathery skin. It can also be cooked just slightly until it can be removed from the shell.

If you buy the meat fresh out of the shell, it should be pale gray or tan in color. In shell or out, fresh conch meat should be used within 24 hours.

Conch meat is fairly tough and you'll need to tenderize it, either with lime juice or by hammering it. You can also buy meat frozen (use it within a week) or canned.

Conch can be used for soups, stews, sauces, chowders, and fritters. Figure on two conchs per person or one pound for six people when used as part of a recipe.

Be adventurous—it's a taste you won't soon forget!

Pappas' Marinated Conch

Even though the conch (say "konk") is cut into small pieces, you CANNOT skip the tenderizing process. This makes a good appetizer.

5 pounds conch, out of shell
1 quart lemon juice
2 large white onions, chopped
1 bunch celery, chopped
3 tablespoons white pepper
3 tablespoons salt
4 limes, squeezed
4 ounces vegetable oil

1. Clean and tenderize the conch and then cut into small pieces.

2. Combine all ingredients in a glass bowl.

3. Cover and chill for at least 4 hours before serving.

SERVES: 10 TO 20
PREPARATION TIME: 20 MINUTES, PLUS TIME FOR TENDERIZING AND CHILLING

LOUIS PAPPAS' RIVERSIDE RESTAURANT, TARPON SPRINGS

Siple's 30-Day Marinated Conch

Serve as an appetizer. Don't cheat on the time; wait the 30 days...it's worth it.

5 pounds conch, cleaned
2¹/2 cups cider vinegar
¹/4 cup salt
³/4 cup extra virgin olive oil
12 cloves garlic
Feta cheese
Greek olives
Salonika peppers

We have taken the liberty of quoting Dick Siple's delightful directions verbatim.

1. First pound conch. This is the secret to making it edible. Use the pointed side of a meat hammer. Pound unmercifully 'til the muscle portion is riddled with holes. Give special attention to the thicker portion of the muscle.

2. After your arm recovers from the pounding, boil a gallon of water. Add salt and conch. Cover and lower heat to maintain a steady boil. Allow to cook for 40 minutes, moving conch around occasionally.

3. Remove and cool. Place the cooked conch into sterilized glass jars.

4. Add vinegar, extra virgin olive oil, and water. Peel and bruise 12 cloves of garlic and drop in. Cover tightly. Shake well to mix. Set in refrigerator for at least 30 days. Shake one time a week—DO NOT GET IMPATIENT. It will be ready in 30 days, no less.

5. Cut in julienne* strips when ready. Serve with the feta, olives, and peppers.

* SEE GLOSSARY

SERVES: A LOT OF PEOPLE
PREPARATION TIME: AS LONG AS IT TAKES TO TENDERIZE THE CONCH, PLUS 30 DAYS IN THE REFRIGERATOR
COOKING TIME: 40 MINUTES

Siple's Garden Seat, Clearwater

Bagatelle's Bahamian Cracked Conch

USA Today thought this was heavenly. So did I. Enjoy this feast on the porch of the Bagatelle, overlooking the festivities of Duval Street! Pick up a T-shirt while you're at it.

4   4- to 6-ounce conch steaks, well tenderized

4 cups herbed (with salt, pepper, thyme, pinch baking powder) all-purpose flour for dredging

6 eggs

2 cups milk

3/4 cup clarified butter*

1/2 cup lime juice, Key limes preferred

1. Tenderize conch steak with kitchen-type hammer until the conch doubles in size. This will take at least 10 minutes.

2. Dredge steak in herbed flour, then dip in egg wash made by mixing eggs with milk. Dredge back in flour while heating butter.

3. Sauté conch in butter for 30 seconds over high heat. Turn. Lower heat. Add Key lime juice and serve.

* SEE GLOSSARY

SERVES: 4
PREPARATION TIME: 20 TO 30 MINUTES
COOKING TIME: 5 MINUTES

BAGATELLE, KEY WEST

Pier House Key West Conch Salad

Enjoy this at home or overlooking the beautiful water at The Pier House restaurant in Key West.

1 cucumber, peeled and seeded
1 pound conch steaks
$1/2$ red onion
$1/2$ red pepper
$1/2$ cup cilantro, or Chinese parsley or coriander
Juice of 6-8 Key limes
1 cup extra virgin olive oil
1 teaspoon leaf oregano
1 teaspoon sugar
$1/2$ teaspoon salt
$1/2$ teaspoon ground black pepper

1. Chop conch in $1/8$-inch pieces, cover with lime juice. Marinate for 24 hours. Drain.

2. Chop onions, cucumbers, cilantro, and bell pepper finely. Combine all ingredients. Refrigerate for 24 hours.

SERVES: 4
PREPARATION TIME: 10 MINUTES
REFRIGERATE AND MARINATE: 48 HOURS

THE PIER HOUSE, KEY WEST

Cracked Conch for Two

Simple preparations are often the best. The folks at this long-gone Florida eatery sold a ton of these in their day. Be sure to beat the heck out of the steaks with a heavy mallet!

4 large conch steaks
4 eggs, beaten
1 cup all-purpose flour
Salt and cracked black pepper to taste
Vegetable oil

1. Remove meat from shells. Pound until very tender, about 10 minutes or longer.

2. Dip conch in egg. Roll in flour seasoned with salt and cracked black pepper to taste.

3. Fry in oil at low heat until brown on both sides.

SERVES: 4
PREPARATION TIME: 20 TO 30 MINUTES
COOKING TIME: 20 MINUTES

BIMINI SEA SHACK, FORT LAUDERDALE

King and Queen Conch

Conch Fritters

Make the sauce a few hours in advance so it can mellow. Even though the conch is finely chopped (we did it in a food processor), you MUST tenderize it first. The sauce also may be used for ribs or shrimp.

2 cups self-rising flour
2 cups conch, tenderized and finely chopped
1 large onion, diced
1 green pepper, diced
Salt and pepper
2 dashes Tabasco sauce
2 eggs, lightly beaten
3/4 cup milk, or more

1. Combine all of the above ingredients with enough milk for the mixture to hold its shape. Form into fritters and fry in 350° F. oil until golden.

2. Drain on paper towels and serve with the sauce below or sauce of your choice.

HOT SAUCE

24 ounces catsup
1/4 cup Worcestershire sauce
3 Datil peppers, or any very hot peppers, finely chopped

1. Combine all of the ingredients. Makes 1 quart and will keep in a covered glass jar for a week or two.

SERVES: 4 TO 6
PREPARATION TIME: 30 MINUTES
COOKING TIME: APPROXIMATELY 20 MINUTES

VILANO SEAFOOD SHACK, ST. AUGUSTINE

Big MacGator

Et Cetera – Alligator

A Dish with Bite

You can find alligators just about anywhere in Florida—in freshwater lakes, rivers, residential ponds and canals, along the highways and even in swimming pools. But don't try to catch your own. (There are laws regulating hunting seasons.) Alligators have a natural fear of humans, but will attack if provoked. These reptiles, which can grow up to 14 feet long, have extremely powerful jaws. They also have amazing, but short, bursts of speed. Admire them in the wild, but from a distance.

Alligator meat is low in calories and fat. A 100-gram serving has about 140 calories, sixty-five milligrams of cholesterol and only 3 percent fat. All of the meat, including the tail, is edible and sold in restaurants throughout Florida.

The meat comes in three types: white tail meat is tender, like veal; pinkish body meat has a stronger flavor and a slightly tougher texture; and dark tail meat is suitable only for braised dishes.

Turtle

A Snappy Treat

Turtle fanciers say the greenish meat from the tops of turtle shells is considered to be the tastiest. And the meat from females is more tender than that of males. Turtle meat is used mainly for soups and stews, but also for "turtleburgers."

You probably will only find turtle meat canned. At one time there was a great deal of commercial turtle fishing done in Key West. Now, turtles are protected by a variety of regulations. It's also illegal to disturb the eggs you might find on the beach during nesting season.

Turtle can be enjoyed many ways. Try it sautéed with mushrooms, onions, and green peppers!

Eel

Slippery, but Succulent

Most Americans look upon eel with less than gustatory glee. But those who have tried eel find it really is delicious. Eel is a true member of the fish family and can be caught in all seasons. Most varieties breed in the saltwater of the Atlantic near the coast of Bermuda. The eggs float to their various destinations, hatching as elvers, and make their homes in rivers, streams, ponds, and swamps.

Eels live about ten years, growing from inch-long elvers to as long as ten feet and 170 pounds. The most tasty meat is found in eels weighing 2 pounds or less. The meat is flavorful, rich, and fatty. A 100-gram fillet of eel will have about 180 calories, 12 grams of fat, and 130 milligrams of cholesterol.

Live Wires

If you're in a fishing mood, you can catch eel yourself in a number of ways. You can spear them using underwater lights, fish for them using a sinker that will rest on the bottom, or use eel traps. Check with a sporting goods store about the method that would work best for you.

Not feeling fishy? You still want to get them while they're moving. Buy your eel live at your local market and have it killed on the spot. Let your fish dealer skin and gut it for you (it's a messy job). Eel that's sold pre-skinned or filleted will have lost its freshness.

Eel is particularly good smoked or pickled. It can also be sautéed, broiled, grilled, or added to a stew or soup. Figure on a half-pound per person and use the eel within a day of purchase (or catch).

Snails

Time After Time

You would expect these slow-moving creatures to have plodded their way through history. Evidence suggests the ancient Romans were big fans of these pokey mollusks. The Romans even arranged special vineyards to feed and fatten the snails, pampering them with special foods (such as spicy soups, bay, and wine) so they would be pre-seasoned.

It's not much different today. Most of the snails you'll buy in the market or eat in a restaurant have been raised on special "snail ranches," and are not just plucked from the garden. They go through a lengthy process of fasting, soaking, and rinsing—which takes weeks. And after all that, they still must be soaked in warm water, boiled in salted water or bouillon and cleaned.

Fresh snails are commonplace in French markets. The French are very enthusiastic snail eaters and often purchase them already prepared with garlic butter in their shells, ready for heating. Many French, certainly very patient ones, even catch them and put them through their own ranching and purifying process.

Better Butter

Do yourself a favor, however, and buy the canned variety. Put them in a colander and pour a quart of warm water or a half-cup of wine over them. Drain them, and they are ready for your favorite recipe.

If you love snails, you should find some "escargot" dishes, which are grooved, cupped, and heated to capture the delicious snail butter. Use a spring-handled holder to pick up the snail shell and remove the snail with a small, closely tined fork. Assuredly addictive!

Frog Legs

Catch Them if You Can

In the mood for these tasty treasures? The best time to capture your own is in the spring (they usually hibernate during the winter months). Be on the lookout for bull-frogs (quite large), green or spring frogs (medium), or leopard frogs. These are the most edible species in the United States. If you're quick, you can catch them with your bare hands. You can also try using hook and line, gigs, or clubs. Once you catch them, keep the frogs in a well-ventilated enclosure with a tight top.

As a rule, the only part that is edible is the back legs. Once they're killed, use a pair of scissors to cut the legs as close as possible to the body, making sure the legs are intact. Skinning is done from top to bottom, and it's easier to do if you chill the legs first. Before you include them in any recipe, soak them for at least 2 hours in cold milk, water, or even beer.

Amphibian Adventure

For the less adventurous, edible frogs are commercially grown and sold in fish markets. They're usually sold in pairs, ranging from 2 to 8 ounces. The meat should be white or slightly pink. The meat will keep for up to two days in the refrigerator.

Frozen frog legs are available in many markets, but the usually have lost much of their flavor. Thaw the meat in the refrigerator overnight before cooking. Never thaw at room temperature.

Frog legs have a very delicate flavor and taste best when sautéed, fried, or poached. Because the legs are so fragile, use two large spatulas to turn them while cooking. Cook them briefly. Once overcooked, the meat turns tough. Six small pairs of legs (the most succulent) or three medium will serve one person.

Squid

Inside-Out Shellfish

Squid (better known as calamari on Italian menus) are true mollusks, although they don't look like it because they lack an outer shell. They're also mistaken for octopus, but squid have ten legs, not eight.

Squid are white, covered by a translucent, purplish mottled skin. They swim by jetting water through their bodies, and when they're in danger they squirt ink from their ink sacs. The ink also is used to color pasta, or it can be used in a sauce to accompany seafood.

Worth the Trouble

Squid is high in protein, low in calories and is a good buy—almost all of it is edible. (Two pounds whole will yield 1 1/2 pounds cleaned.)

In the market, fresh squid are sold either cleaned or uncleaned. They should smell of the ocean. Fresh, cleaned squid will last two days in the refrigerator; frozen, one month in the freezer.

To clean squid, remove the spiny translucent portion and then pull the head and legs from the envelope-like covering. Peel the skin from the body and cut across the head above the eyes. (Romangnolis' Table has step-by-step photographs.) Better yet, have your fish dealer clean the squid for you.

Before cooking, squid must be tenderized. It can be fried, stewed, sautéed or poached, stir-fried, or deep-fried. You also may find it sun-dried, canned, or pickled in the market. Make sure you don't overcook squid; it becomes quite rubbery. Just enjoy! Squid could be habit-forming.

Octopus

Decidedly Different

Octopuses, like their squid cousins, are cephalopods (meaning head-legs). They're not really giant creatures from the deep. An octopus is usually one or two feet long and weighs about three pounds.

Fresh and frozen raw octopus is brownish-gray or purplish. If it's fresh, it should still smell of the sea.

The raw octopus you'll find in your market is usually sold whole and cleaned. To clean it yourself, remove the eyes, suckers, ink sac, and mouth; then wash it in several changes of water. Blanch, then remove the skin. The meat will need to be tenderized. Beat it with a mallet or hammer, then cut it into 1-inch pieces before cooking.

Octopus can be stewed, fried, or sautéed according to your favorite recipe. Older and larger octopus will need to cook a little longer. Baby octopus cook quite quickly. You must try this delicious delight!

Silas Dent's Alligator

This was such a delicious and popular dish on St. Pete Beach that Silas Dent's chefs cooked 2,000 pounds of alligator a year for their customers. The original restaurant burned down but there's another ever better, a few blocks from the original.

1 pound alligator meat
4 whole eggs
2 cups beer
1 tablespoon salt
1 tablespoon pepper
1 tablespoon granulated garlic
1 cup milk
Seasoned (with salt, pepper, granulated garlic) self-rising flour
Vegetable oil for frying

1. Cut the alligator meat with the grain into 1-inch strips. Pound to tenderize.

2. Mix the eggs, beer, salt, pepper, and granulated garlic in a glass dish or bowl. Add the alligator meat and marinate for 24 hours in the refrigerator.

3. Mix the flour with the salt, pepper, and granulated garlic. Dip the alligator pieces into the mixture.

4. Heat the oil to 350° F. and fry the strips, moving them around so that they don't stick. It will take about 1 minute to cook. Serve hot.

SERVES: 4
PREPARATION TIME: 20 MINUTES
COOKING TIME: 5 MINUTES
MARINATE: 24 HOURS

SILAS DENT'S RESTAURANT AND OYSTER BAR, ST. PETE BEACH

Fried Alligator

You won't be afraid to get near this gator!

2 pounds alligator meat
5 quarts ice water
Salt and pepper to taste
1 cup all-purpose flour for dredging
Vegetable oil

1. Cut alligator meat into small, finger-sized pieces. Soak the meat in ice water for about 1 hour. Drain.

2. Season to taste with salt and cracked black pepper to taste. Fluff in flour.

3. Deep-fry until done, about 5 minutes, at 340° F.

SERVES: 4
PREPARATION TIME: 10 MINUTES, PLUS SOAKING TIME
COOKING TIME: 5 MINUTES
SOAK: 1 HOUR

THE YEARLING, CROSS CREEK

Gator's Gator Burger

Not your everyday kind of ordinary burger—delicious.

2 to 2¹/₂ pounds alligator meat
¹/₄ pound lean, mild Italian sausage in bulk form
1 to 2 eggs
¹/₂ cup bread crumbs
Salt, pepper, garlic, onion salt to taste

1. Grind alligator meat, normally a tough, fine, and fat-free meat. Add sausage to hold meat together. Work in eggs, bread crumbs, and seasonings to taste. Mix thoroughly.

2. Make patties and grill, preferably on a flat surface indoors. Turn carefully with a spatula to avoid crumbling. Serve on a roll and sink your teeth into the gator!

SERVES: 4 TO 6
PREPARATION TIME: 15 MINUTES
COOKING TIME: 15 TO 20 MINUTES

GATOR GRILL, MARCO ISLAND

Ali - Gator

Angulas De Aguinaga (Baby Eel)

This appetizer is a true delicacy. Baby eels are tiny—only about 1 or 2 inches long-white and very thin. Fresh ones are hard to find. but gourmet and specialty shops occasionally carry them in cans. If you do find them in the market, grab them. You now have the perfect recipe.

10 cloves of garlic, sliced
10 ounces fresh baby eel (may substitute canned eel)
Pinch of fresh chopped parsley
Pinch of crushed red pepper
Few drops of sherry
$^1/_2$ cup extra virgin olive oil
Salt to taste

1. Sauté the garlic in very hot extra virgin olive oil until golden brown. Add the eel, parsley, and red pepper and cook until eel is tender, about 2 to 3 minutes. Stir in the wine and cook for another minute.

2. Serve very, very hot, either in the same dish it was cooked in or in very hot individual serving plates.

SERVES: 2
PREPARATION TIME: 10 MINUTES
COOKING TIME: 4 MINUTES

EL BODEGON DE CASTILLA, MIAMI

Fried Soft-Shell Turtle

This was a great treat at The Yearling. Be sure to visit the house of Marjorie Kinnan Rawlings, author of the Pulitzer Prize-winning novel, *The Yearling*, in Cross Creek.

2 pounds soft-shell turtle * * **meat**
5 to 6 quarts ice water
1 cup all-purpose flour
Vegetable oil for frying

1. Cut meat into 3- or 4-ounce pieces. Soak in ice water for a few minutes. Fluff in flour. Fry in heavy iron skillet until done, about 20 to 25 minutes, turning over once.

** IN MOST PLACES IT IS ILLEGAL TO CATCH MARINE TURTLES. CONSULT YOUR LOCAL COUNTY.

SERVES: 4
PREPARATION TIME: 10 MINUTES
COOKING TIME: 20 TO 25 MINUTES

THE YEARLING, CROSS CREEK

Frog Legs Provençale

Enjoy your frog legs. Be sure to serve with some fresh, steaming veggies!

1/4 pound butter, lightly salted
3 large cloves garlic, chopped
12 large fresh mushrooms
1/2 teaspoon basil, fresh if possible
Freshly ground pepper to taste
12 large pairs frog legs
1 large ripe tomato, chopped
1/3 cup Madeira wine
Juice from 1/2 lemon
Parmesan, freshly grated
Scallions, chopped

1. Melt butter over low heat, very slowly, in a large skillet. Sauté garlic until edges begin to brown. DO NOT BROWN butter. Add mushrooms and sauté 3 to 4 minutes, turning with wooden spoon frequently. Add basil and pepper.

2. Place frog legs in skillet. Add tomatoes and push pieces of tomato into butter.

3. Increase heat and let simmer rapidly for 2 to 3 minutes. Add wine and lemon juice.

4. Turn frog legs over, turning carefully to ensure they remain whole. Cover skillet and reduce heat. Simmer 8 to 10 minutes. DO NOT OVERCOOK.

5. Carefully remove frog legs with tongs and place on serving platter. Cover with gravy remaining in skillet and sprinkle with fresh Parmesan. Garnish with chopped scallions.

SERVES: 4
PREPARATION TIME: 10 MINUTES
COOKING TIME: 20 MINUTES

FROGS LANDING, CEDAR KEY

Pickled Octopus

Serve this as a prelude to an Italian or Greek dinner.

5 pounds octopus
1 quart lemon juice
2 cloves garlic, finely chopped
1 quart white vinegar
3 tablespoons salt
3 tablespoons black pepper
3 teaspoons oregano
$^1/_2$ cup water

1. Clean octopus. Skin and boil, or vice versa, and then chop into small pieces.

2. Mix all ingredients in a glass bowl. Cover and chill for 4 to 6 hours before serving.

SERVES: 10 TO 20
PREPARATION TIME: 30 MINUTES
COOKING TIME: DEPENDS UPON HOW TENDER THE OCTOPUS IS
CHILL: 4 TO 6 HOURS

LOUIS PAPPAS' RIVERSIDE RESTAURANT, TARPON SPRINGS

Half Shell's Squid Rings

Nice consistency! The flavor is unusual—a popular dish at the Half Shell!

2 pounds squid

MARINADE
Juice of 3 Key limes, or may substitute other limes
3 cloves of garlic, crushed and chopped fine
1/2 teaspoon freshly ground black pepper

1. Clean squid. (Remove the spiny translucent portion and then pull head and legs from the envelope-like covering. Peel skin from the body and cut across the head above the eyes.)

2. Cut into 1/2-inch rings. Mix with marinade ingredients and marinate 2 to 3 hours.

BATTER
2 eggs
1 cup milk
1 cup all-purpose flour
1 pound fine cracker meal

1. Prepare an egg wash (eggs and milk mixed). Dust squid with flour, dip in egg wash, then in cracker meal.

2. Refrigerate 1 hour for breading to set.

3. Deep fry to a golden brown.

SERVES: 4 TO 6
PREPARATION TIME: MARINATE 2 TO 3 HOURS, REFRIGERATE 1 HOUR
COOKING TIME: 5 TO 10 MINUTES

HALF SHELL RAW BAR AT LAND'S END VILLAGE, KEY WEST

St. Augustine Squid Sautèed in Garlic

A spicy and quite delicious appetizer. The fresher the squid, the better the squid.

1 to 1¹/₂ cups all-purpose flour
Salt and pepper to taste
2 pounds squid, cleaned, tenderized, and sliced in 1-inch rounds
¹/₂ cup butter
6 scallions, chopped
2 tablespoons chopped chives
4 cloves garlic, finely chopped
¹/₂ cup dry white wine

1. Combine flour, salt, and pepper. Lightly flour the squid.

2. Melt butter and add scallions, chives, and garlic. Sauté until garlic is golden. Add squid and sauté for 5 to 7 minutes or until squid is done. Just before the squid is finished, add the wine and stir.

SERVES: 2
PREPARATION TIME: 15 MINUTES
COOKING TIME: 10 MINUTES

VILANO SEAFOOD SHACK, ST. AUGUSTINE

Escargots Emile

You must have some crusty bread to sop up the sauce, our favorite part of this dish. If you are an escargot fanatic, make a dozen of these just for yourself. Save and thoroughly wash the shells so that next time you can purchase just the snails without the shells.

Garlic butter
24 escargots (snails) and shells, available canned

GARLIC BUTTER
³/₄ pound lightly salted butter, softened
1 teaspoon Italian seasoning
5 cloves garlic, or more for "garlicaholics", minced
3 ounces dry white wine
Pinch of salt
¹/₂ teaspoon black pepper
2 teaspoons all-purpose flour
1 ounce brandy

1. Cream the butter. Add the remaining ingredients, except the snails and shells, and mix well. Refrigerate, but bring to room temperature before using.

2. When ready to cook snails: place a snail and then ¹/₄ teaspoon of garlic butter in each shell. Put on escargot plate, or baking dish, and bake in a 425° F. oven for 15 minutes.

SERVES: 4
PREPARATION TIME: 5 MINUTES
COOKING TIME: 15 MINUTES

CHEZ EMILE, KEY WEST

Empress Lilly Snails in Brioche

The brioche (say BREE-ohsh) can be purchased in many bakeries or supermarkets, or you can make your own. What an elegant combination!

4 brioche shells with the tops removed
20 snails
1/2 cup butter
2 teaspoons shallots
1 teaspoon minced garlic
1 1/3 cups Burgundy, or red wine
2 cups red wine

1. Scoop out a small amount of each brioche.

2. Sauté the snails, shallots, and garlic until the snails are cooked through. Remove from pan. Add the Burgundy and reduce* by one-half. Add red wine and bring to a boil.

3. Place the snails in the brioche, which you have warmed, and pour the sauce over the snails. Place the cap on each brioche and serve immediately.

* SEE GLOSSARY

SERVES: 4
PREPARATION TIME: 15 MINUTES
COOKING TIME: 15 MINUTES

EMPRESS ROOM, EMPRESS LILLY RIVERBOAT,
WALT DISNEY WORLD VILLAGE AT LAKE BUENA VISTA

LONE
SHARK

Shark

Love Me, Love My Shark

Think you've never had shark? Think again. Until it was outlawed, many stores and restaurants offered shark as swordfish, halibut, flounder, and probably other species. Even today you have every right to eye with great suspicion any perfectly formed, perfectly aligned rows of "scallops."

Shark has been popular with Europeans, Africans, and Asians for years. Americans are finally joining the bandwagon, enjoying this light meat with just "moderately" fishy flavor. It doesn't hurt that shark is nutritious and low-calorie, with a lovely lack of bones.

Off the Hook

To get the freshest shark, head to the shark tournaments and wait for the contestants to return. Once the entries have been weighed, you'll probably see marine biologists, restaurateurs, and foodies vying with each other to purchase the shark.

In the market, you'll usually find smaller sharks sold whole. Larger sharks are sold as fillets, steaks, or chunks.

Regardless of where you get it, don't be alarmed if it smells slightly (just slightly) of ammonia. That's its metabolism. You can get rid of the smell by soaking the shark in milk or ice water with a lemon juice or cider vinegar. This will also help firm up the meat. If it smells too much of ammonia, shop around. A strong smell indicates the meat is less than fresh. And if you're not planning on using the meat within 24 hours, freeze it.

If you want to try hooking shark yourself, go with an expert. Shark fishing isn't the same as going after mullet!

Kon Tiki Shark à la Seaport

An unusual preparation for an unusual fish.

2 pounds shark fillets, fresh, if possible
Salt to taste
1 cup all purpose flour, or more, for dredging
4 eggs, beaten
3 to 4 teaspoons clarified butter*
1 cup coconut, shredded
1/2 cup lemon juice, fresh squeezed
Available fresh fruit such as:
Peaches
Apples
Plums
Strawberries
Grapes
Kiwi

1. Slice shark horizontally into 1/4-inch fillets. Flatten each fillet with mallet and lightly salt. Dip into flour and then dip into egg batter.

2. Heat clarified butter* in skillet to 400° F. It must be very hot. Place fillets in skillet and cook until brown. Turn once and brown other side. Remove from skillet and place on serving platter.

3. Add coconut to the remaining butter in skillet.

4. Wash fruit and slice into 1/4-inch pieces. Pat dry. Place fruit into skillet with juices. Sauté very quickly. Add lemon juice to mixture.

5. Pour sauce over fillets. Garnish and serve with potatoes and fresh vegetables.

* SEE GLOSSARY

SERVES: 6 TO 8
PREPARATION TIME: 30 MINUTES
COOKING TIME: 10 TO 15 MINUTES

SEAPORT INN, NEW PORT RICHEY

Silas Dent's Shark

The seasonings can be adjusted to suit your taste. This is a very simple-to-prepare dish and will probably make a shark fan out of anyone who tastes it!

1 1/2 to 2 pounds shark
Oil for searing
Salt, pepper, granulated garlic to taste
3/4 pound butter
2 ounces lemon juice
Rind from 1 lemon
2 teaspoons minced fresh garlic
1 cup vermouth
2 cups dry white wine or water

1. Cut the shark, with the grain, into 4 pieces, approximately 8 or 9 ounces each. Rub with salt, pepper, and granulated garlic to taste, on both sides.

2. Heat a little oil in a frying pan. When it is very hot, place in the shark and sear it on both sides. Remove from the pan and set aside.

3. Mix together the butter, lemon juice, lemon rind, and garlic. Add the vermouth and wine or water and mix well.

4. Place the shark pieces in an oven-proof pan or dish. Pour the butter-wine mixture over the shark. Broil on one side only, about 6 to 8 minutes. Watch the cooking carefully so that the shark does not dry out. The liquids in the pan will cook the underside.

SERVES: 4
PREPARATION TIME: 20 MINUTES
COOKING TIME: 6 TO 8 MINUTES

SILAS DENT'S RESTAURANT AND OYSTER BAR, ST. PETE BEACH

SUSHI

Sushi

If you knew sushi, like I know sushi...

This marriage of fish and rice can be habit-forming (some people actually have withdrawal symptoms from going without it too long!). Sushi is more than just "raw fish." The center of a sushi roll is a combination of raw or cooked seafood or vegetables (called tane) and boiled rice that is formed into decorative, edible packages. The rice is flavored with vinegar and mirin, a sweet rice wine.

The most popular forms of sushi found in the United States are nigiri and forms of rolled sushi. Hand-shaped nigiri has tane place on top of small, oblong portions of rice. Rolled sushi (makizushi) is made by laying a sheet of thin dry nori (seaweed) on a bamboo mat and spread it with rice. The seafood or vegetables are place on top, and the seaweed is rolled into a cylinder. The roll is then cut into pieces and served.

Sushi is the perfect finger food, designed as an appetizer, snack, or full meal. Soy sauce and wasabi (Japanese horseradish) come with the sushi as dipping sauces. By custom, sushi should be eaten in one or two bites. Other garnishes include whisper-thin scallion slices and freshly sliced ginger.

Like sashimi (thinly sliced raw fish), sushi preparation is truly an art. Sushi and sashimi chefs can train for six years.

Sushi Varieties

Anago: A type of sea eel (boiled in seasoned stock, then grilled); a thick, sweet sauce is brushed on just before serving.

Chirashi Sushi: Bed of vinaigrette rice with other ingredients mixed on top.

Dichi Make: Vinaigrette rice, center of avocado, crab meat, pickled daikon radish strip, rolled in seaweed. This sushi variety was named after the sushi cook at the Hyatt Regency Tampa, Dichi.

Ebi: Boiled shrimp.

Kappa Maki: Cucumber-filled, rolled sushi.

Maguro: Red meat of tuna (usually the first raw fish Westerners try, quite similar to rare steak in taste)

Makizushi: Rolled sushi with narrow strips of seafood and crisp vegetables, pickles, or seafood layered with vinaigrette rice.

Nari Sushi: Bean curd pocket filled with a mixture of vinaigrette rice and chopped Oriental relish topped with Kampyo.

Nigiri Sushi: "Sushi" commonly refers to nigiri sushi. Handmade sushi made with a ball of rice and a slice of fish or other topping.

Tamago: Thick omelet sweetened with sugar and mirin, cut in slices and served on rice.

Gari (Pickled Ginger)

A most unusually refreshing taste! You can purchase gari but it is best fresh.

¹/₂ pound ginger root
Salt to taste
1 cup rice vinegar
7 tablespoons water
2¹/₂ teaspoons sugar
Salt

1. Thoroughly wash, peel, and salt fresh ginger root. Let stand one day.

2. Wash again and place in marinade of rice vinegar, water, and sugar. Marinate for 1 week.

3. Drain, cover, and refrigerate. Gari will keep for months.

4. Slice very thin and serve small amount with sushi.

YIELD: APPROXIMATELY ¹/₂ POUND GINGER ROOT
PREPARATION TIME: 20 MINUTES
MARINATE: 8 DAYS

Sushi Rice

Be sure to keep rice from drying out, as proper moistness is a must for good sushi!

3¹/₂ cups short-grain rice, washed
4 cups water
3-inch square giant kelp (konbu), available at Asian food markets
5 tablespoons plus 1 teaspoon rice vinegar**
¹/₃ cup sugar
1 tablespoon sea salt, available at most gourmet specialty shops

CONTINUED...

1. Place rice in heavy-bottomed, medium-sized pot or rice cooker. Add the water.

2. Clean kelp by wiping with damp cloth. More flavors will be released if the kelp is slashed in a few places. Place on top of rice in water. Cover and heat over medium heat just until the boiling point. When just boiling, remove kelp and discard.

3. Cover tightly, boil over high heat for 2 minutes, then turn heat down to medium and boil for 5 minutes. Reduce heat to very low and cook for 15 minutes, or until all the water has been absorbed. Turn heat off and let stand on burner, with pot lid wrapped in a kitchen towel, for 10 to 15 minutes.

4. Dissolve sugar and salt in the vinegar, stirring over low heat. Force-cool to room temperature by placing hot vinegar mixture in a metal bowl and twirling the bowl in a bath of water and ice.

5. Use a flat wooden spoon or proper rice paddle to spread the hot rice in a thin layer in a wide and shallow wooden or plastic bowl. Toss with horizontal, cutting strokes to separate the grains. Use only a sideways cutting motion when mixing.

6. Pour the vinegar mixture generously over the rice. You may not have to use all the vinegar dressing. Be careful not to add too much liquid, which will cause the rice to become mushy.

7. As you toss the rice, cool it quickly and thoroughly by fanning it with a folded newspaper or your hand. It will be easier if you can have someone else standing by to do this. The tossing and cooling should take about 10 minutes. Taste test to see if the rice is at room temperature.

NOTE: VINEGARED RICE SHOULD BE EATEN THE SAME DAY IT IS PREPARED—IT DOES NOT KEEP MORE THAN 1 DAY. DO NOT REFRIGERATE! PLACE THE VINEGARED RICE IN A CONTAINER WHEN IT HAS COOLED TO ROOM TEMPERATURE, THEN COVER WITH A DAMP CLOTH TO KEEP IT FROM DRYING OUT.

** THE FLAVOR OF SUSHI RICE VARIES SOMEWHAT WITH THE SEASONS. A LITTLE MORE VINEGAR MAY BE USED IN THE SUMMER. ADJUST THE FLAVOR OF THE RICE TO SUIT YOUR TASTE.

YIELDS: APPROXIMATELY 10 CUPS
PREPARATION TIME: 1 HOUR
COOKING TIME: 30 TO 40 MINUTES

Westwind'r Sushi Bar at the Hyatt Regency, Tampa

Key West Roll

The sesame seeds add a nice flavor to what other sushi bars call "California Roll"!

Nori, a seaweed, found in Asian food markets
Vinegar and water
Sushi rice (see recipe, page 216)
Sesame seeds
Wasabi, Japanese horseradish found in Asian food markets
    (see recipe, page 219)
Crab cake, found in most seafood stores
Avocado
Cucumber

1. Place sheet of nori on a bamboo sushi mat, available at Asian food markets. Moisten hands with vinegar water.

2. Place rice, the size of a lemon, in middle of nori. Spread evenly from left to right. Sprinkle sesame seeds on rice.

3. Put sheet of plastic wrap over rice mixture. Flip so rice will be on bottom, resting on bamboo mat.

4. Spread a dash of wasabi across the middle of the nori.

5. Place 2 small slices of avocado, one piece of crab cake, and one piece of thinly sliced cucumber across the middle of the nori.

6. Starting on the edge closest to you, use the mat to roll up the sushi.

7. Remove roll from bamboo mat. Remove plastic wrap. Cut the roll in half using a wet knife dipped in vinegar water. Cut each half into 3 equal pieces.

8. Serve with wasabi and pickled ginger.

SERVES: 1 ROLL SERVES 1 PERSON
PREPARATION TIME: 5 MINUTES

KYUSHU RESTAURANT-SUSHI BAR, KEY WEST

Wasabi (Japanese Horseradish)

Powerful...great flavor, it will definitely clean out your sinuses!

1 can powdered wasabi, available in Asian food markets
Water

1. Mix wasabi with small amount of tepid water.

2. Allow to stand for 10 minutes before using.

YIELD: DEPENDS ON AMOUNT OF POWDERED WASABI
PREPARATION TIME: 5 MINUTES

Sushi Shrimp

EMMERT

POTPOURRI

Casseroles
Medleys
Mixed Grills

There is nothing quite like a fine potpourri of Underwater delights. Truly, they "dance" well together in the choreography of fine, delicious cuisine.

Combining varieties of different finfish and shellfish is a skill that only gets better with practice. Who would have thought such combinations possible. Lobster and oysters; yellowtail, scallops and crab; crabmeat and anchovies; ham and shrimp. Odd bedfellows, but the list goes on.

As there are as many recipes for Cuban home cooked beans as there are Cubans, there are inexhaustible combinations of fish and shellfish and other ingredients. In this chapter I have included a selection of the best I have discovered in my twenty-six years in Florida. I have collected them from friends, chefs, cooks, seafood restaurants and others, Southern style food emporiums, roadside buffets, and down-home Ma and Pa eateries.

One of the best recipes is the savory Jambalaya from Vinton's Restaurant in Lake Wales, Florida. There is also a delectable Drunken Casserole made with fine bourbon from The Sovereign in Gainesville and a Zuppa di Pesce from a local chef that would rival any in Naples (Italy, that is).

Add a few of your own touches if you desire, but most of all enjoy!

Oyster and Lobster Cuisine Nouvelle

This recipe was published in one of the first series of Time-Life Books. The chef and I were thrilled. We had fun preparing this for hundreds of Florida aficionados.

4 to 6 Maine lobsters or Florida lobster tails
12 to 15 oysters, shucked
1 peeled carrot, cut in julienne*
1 leek, cut in julienne
6 tablespoons butter
4 shallots
1 tablespoon oil
2 ounces brandy
1 bunch parsley, 1/2 chopped and 1/2 for garnish
1 1/2 cups whipping cream
Salt and pepper to taste

1. Parboil lobster tails. Remove meat. Cut in cubes and set aside.

2. Sauté carrots and leeks in 2 tablespoons butter for 2 minutes. Remove from pan.

3. Sauté shallots in oil in same pan for 2 minutes. Add lobster cubes and oysters. Stir until seared. Remove contents from pan.

4. Flambé* residue carefully with brandy. Add chopped parsley and cream. Season with salt and cracked black pepper to taste and reduce*. Add 4 tablespoons butter and stir until smooth and creamy. Add lobster and oysters. Simmer 1 minute.

5. To serve, pour on serving plate. Sprinkle julienne* vegetables on top. Garnish with parsley sprigs.

* SEE GLOSSARY

SERVES: 6
PREPARATION TIME: 15 MINUTES
COOKING TIME: 20 MINUTES

VINTON'S, CORAL GABLES

Seafood Venetian

You're "gondola" like this one! Use unsalted butter for best results.

8 ounces thick béchamel sauce*
10 ounces fresh snapper fillet or other firm white fish
10 ounces shrimp, 21 to 25 per pound size
10 ounces sea scallops
5 ounces king crab leg meat
1/4 cup butter
1 cup mushrooms, sliced
1 clove garlic, minced
1/4 cup clam juice
2 ounces dry white wine
Salt, pepper, lemon juice to taste

1. Prepare the béchamel sauce and keep warm.

2. Remove all the bones from the snapper and cut into 1-ounce pieces.

3. Peel, devein, and butterfly the shrimp.

4. Wash the scallops and pat dry.

5. Pick over the crab carefully for bits of shell.

6. Melt the butter in a large skillet and sauté the snapper, shrimp, and scallops until almost done. Remove from skillet.

7. Into the same skillet, place the mushrooms and garlic and sauté for 1 minute. Then add the clam juice, dry white wine, and béchamel sauce. Reduce* mixture until thick. Season with salt, pepper, and lemon juice to taste.

8. Add the sautéed snapper, shrimp, and sea scallops to the sauce. Add the crab and simmer for 2 minutes.

9. Serve over rice pilaf.

* SEE GLOSSARY

SERVES: 4
PREPARATION TIME: 20 MINUTES
COOKING TIME: 10 MINUTES

VILLA NOVA, WINTER PARK

Captain's Salad

Great with a Roquefort or oil and balsamic vinegar dressing. A perfect summertime treat redolent of the sea.

1 head iceberg lettuce, medium
1 head romaine lettuce, medium
³/₄ pound fresh lump crab meat or Alaskan king crab meat
³/₄ pound cooked small shrimp, peeled and deveined
¹/₂ cup thinly sliced radishes
2 stalks celery, finely diced
1 medium onion, finely diced
1 medium green pepper, finely diced
¹/₂ cup black olive pieces
4 anchovy fillets

1. Wash and tear iceberg and romaine lettuce. Drain well and mix together. Place in a large wooden bowl, peaking slightly in the center.

2. Divide the bowl into 6 equal wedges, like slices of a pie. On opposite wedges place the crab meat and the shrimp, leaving the center of the bowl open for the sliced radishes.

3. In 2 other opposite wedges spread the diced celery and onions. In the last 2 wedges spread the diced green pepper and black olive pieces. Top with anchovy fillets.

4. Toss with your favorite dressing.

SERVES: 4 TO 6
PREPARATION TIME: 20 MINUTES

THE CAPTAIN'S TABLE, DEERFIELD BEACH

Pâté Neptune

This is a very impressive-looking dish to set before your most sophisticated friends. Keeps for 2 to 3 days in the refrigerator. Take on the boat with you and produce at cocktail time to wow your sailing pals.

CRÊPES
- 1/2 **cup all-purpose flour**
- **1 egg**
- 3/4 **cup milk**
- 1/2 **teaspoon salt**
- **2 tablespoons butter**

1. Combine flour, egg, milk, salt, and 1 tablespoon melted butter to make crêpes.

2. Make crêpes in butter in a 5-inch crêpe pan and set aside.

COLD SAUCE 1
- **Mayonnaise**
- **Watercress**
- **Spinach**
- **A little sour cream**

1. Process all together. Create to your own taste.

COLD SAUCE 2
- **1 large tomato, seeded and coarsely chopped, about 1 cup**
- 1/2 **teaspoon paprika**
- **Dash of cayenne**
- **1 teaspoon salt**
- 1/4 **teaspoon white pepper**
- **1 tablespoon good red wine vinegar**
- **1 egg yolk**
- **1 cup vegetable or olive oil**

1. Combine all ingredients except the oil in the container of a food processor. Blend 30 to 40 seconds until smooth. With motor still running, add oil slowly, about 15 to 20 seconds. Taste for seasonings. If too thick, add 1 to 2 tablespoons lukewarm water until it is a creamy consistency.

CONTINUED...

FILLING

¹/₄ pound spinach

1 pound boneless skinless salmon

1 pound scallops

1 pound boneless skinless halibut

2 cups heavy cream

3 egg whites

³/₄ teaspoon salt per pound of fish

¹/₄ teaspoon white pepper each for scallops and halibut

¹/₄ teaspoon cayenne pepper for salmon

1. Blanch* spinach and cool.

2. Put very cold salmon in the container of a food processor. Start motor and add 1 egg white, ³/₄ cup cream, ³/₄ teaspoon salt, and ¹/₄ teaspoon cayenne pepper. Process, then remove and put aside.

3. Put very cold scallops in processor. Start motor and add 1 egg white, ³/₄ cup heavy cream, ³/₄ teaspoon salt, ¹/₄ teaspoon pepper. Process, then remove and put aside.

4. Put very cold halibut in processor. Start motor and add 1 egg white, ¹/₂ cup heavy cream; cold, drained spinach; ³/₄ teaspoon salt, and ¹/₄ teaspoon white pepper.

5. Butter a 3¹/₂-pound mold. Line with crêpes. Layer the various colors of the filling in the crêpes; or arrange the fish and spinach so that the colors make a circle in the center of the mold (this takes practice). Be sure to work with dry hands or spatula when layering the purée into the mold.

6. Cover with the crêpes. Place mold in larger pan with hot water halfway up sides of mold.

7. Place in a preheated 250° F. oven. Cook almost 2 hours. Temperature in center should reach 160° F.

8. This can be served hot or cold, but is usually served cold. Serve with one of the cold sauces listed above.

* SEE GLOSSARY

SERVES: 8 TO 10
PREPARATION TIME: 1 HOUR, INCLUDING CRÊPE-MAKING TIME
COOKING TIME: 2 HOURS

SWANSON'S BISTRO AND WINE BAR, CLEARWATER

Treasures of the Sea

The chef explained that saving the "washwater" from the scallops is very important. This "essence of the sea" from the scallops is therefore captured and gives an added flavor to the court-bouillon* and later to the sauce. Try this and you'll see!

1 pound bay scallops

3 cups water

1 sprig of parsley

2 crushed bay leaves

$^1/_2$ medium onion, diced

1 stalk celery, peeled and diced

$^1/_2$ teaspoon white peppercorns

Salt to taste

$^1/_2$ cup butter

$^1/_2$ cup all-purpose flour

$^1/_2$ cup dry white wine

$^1/_2$ cup heavy cream

2 teaspoons lemon juice

Dash of cayenne pepper

8 ounces small shrimp, cooked, peeled, and deveined

8 ounces lump crab meat

8 ounces mushrooms, sliced and sautéed in butter

4 ounces finely chopped pimientos

4 large shrimp with tails left on, peeled and deveined

Parmesan cheese for garnish

* SEE GLOSSARY

CONTINUED...

1. Wash the scallops in 1 or 2 cups of water. Strain and save this "washwater".

2. In a saucepan, place water, parsley, crushed bay leaves, onion, celery, peppercorns, and salt to taste. Bring to a boil. Add the "washwater" and simmer slowly until a good stock flavor is reached, about 15 to 20 minutes. Strain this court-bouillon*.

3. Preheat the oven to 400° F.

4. In another saucepan, melt the butter and stir in the flour. When all flour has been absorbed into the butter, add about 2 cups of the court-bouillon, stirring constantly.

5. Remove the sauce from the heat and beat vigorously with a wire whisk or electric mixer. Add wine. Beat in the heavy cream, lemon juice, and cayenne. Continue beating until cool.

6. Mix the scallops, small shrimp, crab meat, mushrooms, and pimientos in a large bowl. Divide into 4 casserole dishes. Top each with a large shrimp in the center. Cover with the sauce. Sprinkle with Parmesan cheese.

7. Bake until bubbling, about 10 minutes.

* SEE GLOSSARY

SERVES: 4
PREPARATION TIME: 30 MINUTES
COOKING TIME: 30 TO 40 MINUTES

THE CAPTAIN'S TABLE, DEERFIELD BEACH

Driftwood's Eggplant, Shrimp, and Crab Meat

You can use all crab meat or all shrimp if you wish. "Sea legs" (imitation crab meat) can be substituted for crab meat. Best when made several hours before serving so that the flavors get a chance to meld. Bring to room temperature before baking. You might want additional Tabasco or Worcestershire in the recipe, but DO NOT use LESS than what is called for.

2 medium eggplant, peeled and cut into large cubes
2 tablespoons butter
2 onions, chopped
2 bell peppers, chopped
2 cloves garlic, chopped
1 1/2 ribs celery, chopped
1 pound crab meat, picked over
1 pound raw shrimp, shelled and deveined and then barely cooked
4 ounces Parmesan cheese
1/4 cup Worcestershire sauce
10 drops Tabasco sauce
1 2/3 cups cooked rice
Salt and pepper to taste

1. Melt butter. Sauté onions, peppers, garlic, and celery until onion is translucent.

2. Soak eggplant in salt water for 30 minutes. Drain, rinse, and steam for 12 minutes or until soft.

3. Combine all ingredients but reserve half of the Parmesan.

4. Taste for seasonings. Put into casserole dish and top with the remaining Parmesan.

5. Bake in a 350° F. oven for 30 minutes or until heated through.

SERVES: 6
PREPARATION TIME: 30 MINUTES
COOKING TIME: 12 MINUTES FOR EGGPLANT, 3 MINUTES FOR SHRIMP, 30 MINUTES IN OVEN

THE DRIFTWOOD RESTAURANT, PENSACOLA

Drunken Fish Casserole

A seafood lover's feast in one dish. But you will want another!

1/2 **cup butter**
1 **clove garlic, finely crushed**
1 **lobster tail, meat chopped**
8 **medium shrimp, peeled and deveined**
8 **medium clams in shell, well drained (save liquid)**
1/2 **cup bourbon**
2 **cups diced and seeded fresh tomatoes**
1 **cup clam juice**
1/2 **pound red snapper in large cubes**
1/2 **pound flounder in large cubes**
1/2 **pound fresh scallops**
Chopped fresh parsley
Fresh ground pepper to taste
1/4 **cup butter, melted**
Lemon wedges

1. Preheat oven to 350° F.

2. Place a large oven-proof sauté pan on stove and heat until hot. Add 1/2 cup butter and garlic. Quickly rotate pan to coat bottom and sides.

3. Add lobster, shrimp, and clams and toss a couple of minutes. Add bourbon and reduce* liquids. Add tomatoes, clam juice, snapper, flounder, scallops, parsley, pepper. Bring to boil and place in oven for 15 to 20 minutes.

4. Remove from oven. Add 1/4 cup butter and squeeze several lemon wedges over all and mix well. Serve garnished with additional lemon wedges.

* SEE GLOSSARY

SERVES: 6 TO 8
PREPARATION TIME: 15 TO 20 MINUTES
COOKING TIME: 45 MINUTES TO 1 HOUR

THE SOVEREIGN RESTAURANT, GAINESVILLE

Seafood Catalana

This is a hearty and delightful seafood stew. Be sure to serve with crusty French bread and a bottle of dry white wine.

2 tablespoons diced green pepper
1 tablespoon minced garlic
2 tablespoons diced onion
2 tablespoons extra virgin olive oil
1/2 pound scallops
1/2 pound shrimp, shelled and deveined
1/2 pound lobster, cut in bite-size pieces
1/2 pound clams
4 stone crab claws
2 ounces Spanish brandy, warmed
1 10-ounce can stewed tomatoes
1 cup beef consommé
Salt to taste

1. Preheat oven to 400° F.

2. Sauté green pepper, garlic, and onion in extra virgin olive oil for 7 minutes. Add washed and prepared seafood. Flambé* with brandy. Add tomatoes, consommé, and salt.

3. Bake 12 minutes or until seafood is just done.

* SEE GLOSSARY

SERVES: 4
PREPARATION TIME: 20 MINUTES
COOKING TIME: 20 MINUTES

EL BODEGON DE CASTILLA, MIAMI

Mama Mia's Cioppino

A simple variation, this is one of the best you'll ever taste. Be sure to use a great tomato sauce. It's "bellissimo"!

1/3 cup extra virgin olive oil

2 cups chopped onions

3 large cloves garlic, chopped

1/2 cup juice from canned clams

1 1-pound 12-ounce can stewed tomatoes (with celery, green peppers, and onions)

1 cup tomato sauce, preferably homemade

1 teaspoon shrimp base, available at gourmet specialty shops

1/2 teaspoon oregano

1/2 teaspoon basil

1/4 teaspoon pepper

FISH

2 pounds ocean perch

12 pre-cooked shrimp, 16 to 20 per pound size

4 tablespoons "titi" shrimp, or small shrimp, cooked or canned

4 tablespoons chopped clams

8 mussels in shells, steamed just until open

1 to 2 pounds spaghetti, cooked al dente*

1. Heat oil. Add onions and cook until onions are soft. Add next 8 ingredients. Simmer for 30 minutes. Add perch. Cook until done. Remove perch from sauce and set aside.

2. To serve, place the perch, shrimp, titis, and chopped clams on spaghetti. Pour sauce over all.

3. Garnish each plate with two mussels in shell.

* SEE GLOSSARY

SERVES: 4
PREPARATION TIME: 10 MINUTES
COOKING TIME: 50 TO 60 MINUTES

RISTORANTE MAMA MIA, TAMPA

Chef Ponzo's Zuppa di Pesce

Chef Salvatore Ponzo explains that Zuppa di Pesce is a Neapolitan fishermen's dish that gives "the most intense power to the body and plenty of vitamins and proteins to anyone who likes fish and shellfish." Legend has it that the dish originated with Neptune, King of the Sea, who was so much in love with a beautiful goddess that he decided to use all of his skill and resources from his watery dominion to create a special dish to please her. The beautiful goddess was so impressed by the meal that she agreed to become his wife.

2 oysters, shucked

4 little neck clams

12 mussels

1 lobster, split in half

1 cup extra virgin olive oil

4 medium squid, cleaned and cut into small rings

4 smelts, finger size

2 fillets of sole, flounder, or turbot, 4 to 8 ounces each

12 sea scallops

12 bay scallops

12 large shrimp

1 cup Chablis

Few fresh basil leaves

Few capers

Pinch oregano

White pepper to taste

3 tablespoons granulated garlic powder

Crushed red pepper to taste

3 to 5 cups of your favorite marinara sauce

1/2 to 1 pound linguine, cooked al dente*

* SEE GLOSSARY

CONTINUED...

1. Wash all the shellfish well. Shuck the oysters, saving the liquor. Steam open the clams and mussels. Clean the lobster.

2. In a large frying pan, bring oil to a sizzling point. Put in the split lobster and cover. Turn down the heat and cook for a few minutes, "trembling" the pan so that the lobster doesn't stick. Remove the cover and add the squid. Very, very delicately, add the clams and mussels in their shells, the shucked oysters, smelts, sole, scallops, and shrimp. Add the wine, the oyster liquor, basil, capers, oregano, pepper, granulated garlic powder, and crushed red pepper.

3. Cover and simmer for 20 minutes. Make sure to "tremble" the pan often so the fish doesn't stick to the bottom. This applies particularly when you are cooking with electric heat, which tends to stay hotter than gas. Watch the pan carefully.

4. Add the marinara sauce and finish cooking slowly until the entire sauce becomes thick.

5. Put the linguine in a large serving dish. Starting with the shellfish, arrange all the fish on top of the linguine in an attractive pattern.

SERVES: 2 TO 4
COOKING TIME: APPROXIMATELY 30 MINUTES

THE SEAPORT CHEF, ST. PETERSBURG

Shrimp and Scallop Mardi Gras

Vermouth is white wine that has been fortified and flavored with spices and herbs. Try the Bianco style for this fricassee of shrimp and scallops. The flavor is light and mild. For variety, you may wish to add oregano or dill.

2 pounds medium large shrimp, peeled and deveined
2 pounds fresh bay scallops
4 ounces butter
1 cup diced red peppers
1 cup diced tomatoes
1/2 cup minced green onions
1 teaspoon minced garlic
1 teaspoon basil
Salt, pepper, and lemon juice to taste
1 cup vermouth
1 teaspoon beurre manié*
1/2 cup chopped parsley

1. Sauté shrimp and scallops in butter for 3 minutes over high heat. Add red peppers, tomatoes, green onions, garlic, basil, salt, pepper, lemon juice, and vermouth. Cook 3 to 4 minutes.

2. Stir in beurre manié with a whisk. Add chopped parsley and serve immediately.

* SEE GLOSSARY

SERVES: 8
PREPARATION TIME: 30 MINUTES
COOKING TIME: 8 TO 9 MINUTES

BON APPETIT, DUNEDIN

Fettuccine Fruites des Mer

There's just enough sauce in this dish to enhance the shrimp and scallops without overpowering their wonderfully delicate flavor. Serve as an appetizer or as a main dish.

1 pound fettuccine, cooked al dente*
12 shrimp, 16 to 20 per pound size
1 pound scallops
3 cloves garlic, minced
1/3 cup extra virgin olive oil
1/3 cup dry white wine
1/3 cup fish stock or clam juice
1/4 cup lemon juice, freshly squeezed
Pinch white pepper
Pinch rosemary
Pinch basil
1/3 pound Romano cheese, freshly grated

1. Cook fettuccine. Put in a warm serving dish; set aside, keeping warm.

2. Heat extra virgin olive oil in a sauté pan until aroma can be sensed. Add scallops and shrimp and sauté until firm. Remove from pan.

3. Add dry white wine to pan to deglaze*. Add garlic, lemon juice, and stock. Season with white pepper, basil, and rosemary. Stir and cook slightly. Return shrimp and scallops to pan and stir gently.

4. Pour over fettuccine and garnish with Romano cheese. Serve immediately.

* SEE GLOSSARY

SERVES: 4 TO 6
PREPARATION TIME: 1 HOUR, INCLUDING TIME TO CLEAN SHRIMP
COOKING TIME: 15 MINUTES

BROTHERS, TOO, TAMPA

Bentley's Seafood Linguine

A rich but delicate sauce complements the shellfish.

VELOUTÉ SAUCE
- 2/3 **cup butter**
- 1/2 **cup all-purpose flour**
- 3 **tablespoons minced shallots**
- 1 **tablespoon minced garlic**
- 1 **quart fish stock***
- 6 **eggs**
- 2 1/2 **cups heavy cream**
- 2 **tablespoons Dijon mustard**
- **Salt and pepper to taste**

1. Sauté shallots and garlic in 2 tablespoons of butter until golden. Set aside.

2. Melt 8 tablespoons of butter and stir in the flour. Cook until slightly brown. Stir in fish stock, little by little, and continue to stir until thickened. Add reserved garlic and shallots.

3. Quickly whisk the eggs into the heavy cream and then whisk into the thickened sauce. Add mustard, salt, and pepper to taste.

* SEE GLOSSARY

CONTINUED...

2/3 cup butter

4 4-ounce lobster tails, cleaned and shelled

12 large shrimp, peeled and deveined

2 cups diced clams, fresh or canned, rinsed and drained if canned

16 medium asparagus spears, fresh or frozen

2 tablespoons brandy

1/2 cup freshly grated Parmesan cheese

1 pound linguine, cooked al dente*

1. Melt 6 tablespoons of butter in a heavy pan. Add lobster and shrimp and cook over a low heat for 2 to 3 minutes. Add diced clams and cook for 2 more minutes. Pour brandy over seafood and flambé*.

2. Toss linguine with 4 tablespoons melted butter and salt and cracked black pepper to taste.

3. Pour Velouté Sauce over the noodles, toss, and simmer for 5 minutes.

4. Steam asparagus until tender.

5. To serve: divide noodles equally onto 4 plates and top each portion with seafood, asparagus, and sauce. Pass Parmesan separately.

* SEE GLOSSARY

SERVES: 4
PREPARATION TIME: 30 MINUTES
COOKING TIME: APPROXIMATELY 30 MINUTES

BENTLEY'S, CLEARWATER

Vinton's Shrimp Jambalaya

This is one of the best jambalayas we've tasted. Vinton's, a classy, classy restaurant in Lake Wales, has been widely acclaimed for this easy but excellent recipe.

1 medium green bell pepper
1 small Spanish onion
2 celery ribs
6 ounces smoked ham
3 large cloves garlic, minced
1/8 cup extra virgin olive oil
12 large shrimp, peeled and deveined
Dash of curry
3 tablespoons Worcestershire sauce
1 16-ounce can whole peeled tomatoes
1/2 cup cooked rice
Salt and pepper to taste

1. Cut pepper, onion, celery, and smoked ham into thin strips.

2. Sauté garlic in oil until golden brown. Add vegetables and ham. Cook for 5 minutes over medium heat. Add raw shrimp, curry, Worcestershire, and tomatoes.

3. Cook for about 10 minutes, or until shrimp are almost done. Add rice, salt, and pepper to taste and cook for 2 minutes longer.

SERVES: 2 TO 4
PREPARATION TIME: 20 MINUTES
COOKING TIME: 20 MINUTES

VINTON'S NEW ORLEANS, LAKE WALES

SOUPS AND CHOWDERS

Soups
and
Chowders

Soups and Chowders have always played a prominent part in my life, especially when my husband Henry and I entertain guests for dinner. In addition to being one of the easiest courses to prepare (making soups *is* an inexact science) soups and chowders are often the most memorable part of the meal. And, best of all, they make for easy entertaining. They can be prepared a day ahead and served the next day when time has melded the fabulous flavors.

For sure, soups reflect the seasons, even here in sunny Florida. Summer soups are made with local oranges, grapefruits and exotic fruits and vegetables from the nearby islands. A hot bowl of steamy fish chowder in the nippy months of December and January takes the chill out of the air. And the fragrant aromas of spring and fall harvests of a mélange of squash and root vegetables are a harbinger of the main feast to follow.

If you're in a party mood, try Cap's Bahamian Party Conch Chowder made with succulent conch meat, which is available today at many seafood stores. For stew aficionados, there is no better or more delicious oyster stew than that made popular at St. Petersburg's famous Derby Lane dog track. And then, of course, there is the remarkable Seafood Bisque from the Don CeSar, the magnificent beach resort on St. Pete Beach.

Whichever you try, be certain to use the best fish stock and freshest ingredients available. Here's wishing you a great Underwater adventure!

Marty's Shellfish Chowder

Serve this in a deep bowl, making sure that everyone gets some fish. This should be served piping hot. The better the bacon, the better the flavor.

1 ounce crab meat, cut in chunks
3 medium shrimp, peeled and deveined
2 mussels, well scrubbed
1 ounce chopped clams
1/4 pound bacon
1/2 cup finely chopped onions
2 cloves garlic, minced
1/4 pound butter
2 cups canned New England clam chowder
2 cups heavy cream
1 teaspoon shrimp base, optional

1. Steam open the shellfish.

2. Cook the bacon to the chewy, not crisp, stage. Drain and dice.

3. Melt butter and sauté onions and garlic until golden. Stir in canned clam chowder, cream, and shrimp base. Cook until blended and hot. Pour over the steamed shellfish and serve with crackers.

SERVES: 4
PREPARATION TIME: 5 MINUTES
COOKING TIME: 10 MINUTES

MARTY'S STEAKS, TAMPA

Florida Fish Chowder

Make this with a variety of fish. The fresher, the better.

1 quart fish or chicken stock*
2 cups finely chopped conch and/or fish
1 cup finely chopped green pepper
1 cup finely chopped celery
1 cup finely chopped onion
3/4 to 1 cup instant potato flour
1 cup milk
1 cup heavy cream
Salt, pepper, Tabasco sauce to taste

1. Sauté all the vegetables and conch/fish without browning them. Add sautéed vegetables to the heated stock and cook over medium heat approximately 10 minutes.

2. Add the instant potato flour, then the milk and the cream. Simmer.

* SEE GLOSSARY

SERVES: 6 TO 8
PREPARATION TIME: 15 MINUTES
COOKING TIME: 30 MINUTES

NEW RIVER STOREHOUSE, FORT LAUDERDALE

Bahamian Party Conch Chowder

This is a double batch–40 or 50 or more bowls, not cups. Chef Steve Knight says it tastes even better the second day it's heated.

1 pound salt pork, chopped
2 pounds butter
4 pounds onions, chopped
4 cups plain all-purpose flour
4 46-ounce cans clam juice
6 quarts fresh clam juice
2 large cans tomato juice
2 #10 cans crushed tomatoes
2 stalks celery, chopped
6 pounds chopped carrots, cooked
12 pounds diced potatoes, cooked
2 tablespoons white pepper
2 tablespoons cayenne red ground pepper
1 fifth sherry wine
8 pounds diced Bahamian conch, tenderized and cooked in pressure cooker for 30 minutes

1. Melt the butter in a very large pan and sauté the onions until golden over medium heat. Stir in the flour and cook until slightly brown. Add the clam juice and tomato juice, a little at a time, stirring constantly.

2. Add the rest of the ingredients and mix. Simmer until the vegetables are tender.

SERVES: A VERY LARGE CROWD
PREPARATION TIME: 1 HOUR
COOKING TIME: 30 TO 60 MINUTES

CAP'S SEAFOOD RESTAURANT, ST. AUGUSTINE

Bentley's Classic New England Clam Chowder

If purchasing clams from your fishmonger, be sure to discard any hard-shell clams, whose open shells will not close when touched. Transplanted New Englanders, and everybody else, will like this creamy chowder. You can substitute margarine for the butter, but it won't taste as good.

1 pound steamed fresh clams
1/4 cup butter, melted
2 cups coarsely chopped celery
5 cups coarsely chopped Spanish onion
2 cloves garlic, crushed
4 crushed bay leaves
1/4 cup butter
1/4 cup all-purpose flour
3 tablespoons clam stock ** mixed with 1 3/4 cups water**
1 tablespoon fresh thyme
1 teaspoon salt or to taste
1 cup white potatoes, peeled, cooked, and diced
1 1/4 cups heavy cream

1. Wash clams thoroughly. Sauté the celery, onion, garlic, and crushed bay leaves in butter until vegetables are tender. Set aside.

2. Melt other 1/4 cup of butter. Stir in flour to make a roux* and stir until it starts to brown. Gradually whisk in clam-water mixture. Stir rapidly until smooth and then simmer for 10 minutes or so, stirring occasionally.

3. Add sautéed vegetables, thyme, and salt to the clam mixture and simmer for 5 minutes. Add clams and potatoes. Gradually add the cream and stir continuously until warm and well mixed.

* SEE GLOSSARY

** MAY USE BOTTLED JUICE OR SEE GLOSSARY FOR DIRECTIONS ON HOW TO PREPARE STOCK.

SERVES: 4
PREPARATION TIME: 20 MINUTES
COOKING TIME: 30 MINUTES

BENTLEY'S, CLEARWATER

Derby Lane's Oyster Stew

Clam "liquor" that is extracted during shucking is sold bottled undiluted as "clam juice" or when diluted as "clam broth." If you purchased oysters out of the shell, be sure to use clam juice for a stronger flavor.

This can be held for several hours without curdling. This is a simple recipe with mouth-watering taste. Serve with cheddar cheese sticks and oyster crackers.

4 cups light cream
3 dozen fresh shucked oysters—save the oyster liquor
1/2 cup dry white wine
2 tablespoons butter
Salt, white pepper, and cayenne to taste
Fresh parsley

1. Poach the oysters in their own liquor and wine until their edges curl and they plump up. Place in a double boiler. Add cream, salt, pepper, and cayenne. Heat until very hot.

2. Add butter and parsley.

SERVES: 6
PREPARATION TIME: 30 MINUTES, INCLUDING SHUCKING
COOKING TIME: 15 MINUTES

DERBY LANE RESTAURANT, ST. PETERSBURG

Chef Watson's Conch Chowder

This recipe was given to me nearly two decades ago by Chef Watson and the folks at the beautiful South Seas Resort on Captiva Island. It is simply delectable; the bacon and vegetables bring out the best of the conch.

The conch for this recipe is tenderized by cooking, not by pounding. You probably will have most of the ingredients on hand, so it is a great recipe to make if you stumble upon some conch on the beach. If you don't, order the conch in 5-pound boxes from your seafood shop.

2 conch, cleaned
1 large onion, diced
1 small onion, diced
3 celery stalks, diced
1 green pepper, diced
1 peeled carrot, peeled and diced
2 strips bacon, diced
1 large potato, peeled and diced
Tabasco sauce to taste
Pinch of thyme
Pinch of basil
3 crushed bay leaves
1 small tomato, diced
Salt and pepper to taste

1. Cover the conch with water and simmer until the conch is tender. The amount of time varies with the size of the conch. Remove from the water and dice. Save the water. Set aside.

2. Sauté the onions, celery, pepper and carrot in a large saucepan along with the bacon until they are crisp-tender.

3. Place sautéed vegetables and bacon, potato, thyme, basil, bay leaves, and conch in a large pot along with the water which you have saved and strained. Simmer until vegetables are very tender, about 30 to 40 minutes. Add tomato and cook for 5 more minutes. Add salt and pepper to taste. Correct seasonings.

SERVES: 4 TO 6
PREPARATION TIME: 20 MINUTES, PLUS CONCH COOKING TIME
COOKING TIME: APPROXIMATELY 40 MINUTES

CHADWICK'S, CAPTIVA ISLAND

Don CeSar Seafood Bisque

The American lobster, a large marine crustacean (Homaris americanus) comes from the Maritime Provinces of Canada, as far north as Belle Isle, to the coastal waters of North Carolina and is most abundant in the waters of Nova Scotia, Newfoundland, and, of course, Maine. Wherever they come from, when you purchase lobster you must enjoy the deliciousness of a fabulous seafood bisque. Like this one, for instance. A real "Lucullan" feast!

LOBSTER ESSENCE

3 8-ounce lobster tail shells
1/2 tablespoon soybean oil
1/2 onion, diced 1/2 inch
1/2 peeled carrot, diced 1/2 inch
1/2 celery stalk, diced 1/2 inch
1/2 large tomato, diced 1/2 inch
Bay leaves
1 1/2 ounces cognac
Salt and whole black pepper to taste
8 ounces fish fumé*

1. Shell the lobster tails and set meat aside.

2. Sauté the diced onions in the hot oil in a large heavy saucepan. Add the lobster shells; flip them over until they become red. Add the carrot, celery, tomato, and bay leaves. Cook for 1 minute.

3. Add the cognac and flambé*. Season with salt and pepper and fish fumé. Bring to boil, remove from heat, and let cool. Strain before serving.

* SEE GLOSSARY

CONTINUED...

LOBSTER

3 8-ounce lobster tails, meat only
1/2 pound "titi" shrimp
1/2 ounce shallots
1 1/2 ounces soybean oil
1 1/2 ounces butter
1/2 ounce cognac
4 tablespoons all-purpose flour
1/2 cup California dry white wine
1 cup fish fumé*
1 cup lobster essence (see recipe above)
5 ounces snow crab meat
1 ounce sherry
1/2 pint heavy cream

1. Using a sharp knife, cut the reserved lobster meat into medallions, 4 per tail.

2. In a hot pot, sauté the shallots. Add the lobster and shrimp. Cook slightly.

3. Deglaze* with the cognac.

4. Add the flour and mix until a thick paste appears. Add the dry white wine, the fish fumé, and the lobster essence. Simmer for 15 minutes, then add the crab meat.

5. Turn off the heat, add the cream and sherry, and serve.

* SEE GLOSSARY

SERVES: 6
PREPARATION TIME: 30 MINUTES
COOKING TIME: 30 MINUTES

King Charles Restaurant at the Don CeSar Resort Hotel, St. Pete Beach

Wine Cellar Spinach & Clam Soup

This is a fresh-tasting soup that is good to serve at any time of the year.
If you wish to substitute fresh clams for canned, wash thoroughly, steam them
open, drain, and chop.

1   6^1/$_2$-ounce can clams, rinsed and drained
^{1}/$_2$ medium onion, diced
4 strips of bacon, diced
4 anchovy fillets, minced
1 clove garlic, minced
1 stick butter
2 tablespoons all-purpose flour
4 cups chicken stock or broth
1   10^1/$_2$-ounce package spinach, thawed and squeezed dry
1 cup heavy whipping cream
Salt and pepper to taste
Pernod, optional

1. Heat a heavy skillet over medium-high heat. Add onion, bacon, anchovies,
    and garlic and sauté lightly. Remove from heat and set aside.

2. Melt the butter in a large saucepan over medium heat. Add flour and stir
    constantly for 2 to 3 minutes. Slowly whisk in stock and bring to a boil.
    Add reserved mixture, spinach, and clams. Bring back to a boil, stirring
    occasionally. Add cream and bring to a boil again.

3. Add salt and cracked black pepper to taste to taste and a dash of Pernod,
    if desired.

SERVES: 6 TO 8
PREPARATION TIME: 10 MINUTES, PLUS THAWING TIME FOR SPINACH
COOKING TIME: 10 TO 15 MINUTES

THE WINE CELLAR RESTAURANT, FORT LAUDERDALE

Brothers' Cold Avocado Crab Soup

Ah, what a welcome relief for a hot summer day in Florida! I love making this with Florida avocados, but Hass will do just fine. Make sure that you make this far enough in advance so that it is very well chilled.

2 Florida or Hass avocados, peeled
1 4-ounce can crab meat, picked over and drained
1/4 cup minced celery
1/2 cup sour cream
1 cup heavy whipping cream
Salt and white pepper to taste
Dash Tabasco sauce
Toasted almonds for garnish

1. Dice one avocado in 1/4-inch cubes. Puree the other one in the container of a blender or food processor.

2. Combine the crab meat, celery, sour cream, heavy cream, salt, and pepper to taste, Tabasco, and the avocados. Mix thoroughly and chill for several hours.

3. If the consistency is too thick, thin with heavy cream. Garnish with toasted almonds.

SERVES: 4 TO 5
PREPARATION TIME: 20 MINUTES
COOKING TIME: 5 MINUTES
CHILL: SEVERAL HOURS

BROTHERS, TOO, TAMPA

EMMERT

SAUCED LOBSTER

Sauces

Fresh fish can only be enhanced by the addition of a delicious and well-made sauce. Whether you make a sauce of sour cream and fresh dill, catsup and fiery peppers, or an exquisite white sauce with fresh fennel, you will want to choose the appropriate sauce that goes best with your choice of seafood.

For stone crabs there are no better condiments than fresh clarified butter and mustard sauce made with fresh mayonnaise, real cream and English-style mustard. With deep-fried fish there are few better sauces than a perfect tartar or a zesty red cocktail. For those of you with a penchant for citrus sauces try Pepin's Orange Mustard sauce, great with fresh fried jumbo shrimp. Your guests will be raving for days!

In Florida, many restaurants have been made famous by serving delectable sauces. O'Steen's in St. Augustine draws daily crowds for a zippy salmon-colored Shrimp Sauce. Joe's Stone Crab on Miami's South Beach is world-famous for Stone Crab Mustard Sauce, and the once renowned (but now closed) Café Chauveron in Bay Harbor Islands will be forever praised for their ethereal Fennel Sauce made with fresh shallots, herbs and fresh cream.

One thing is important to remember when creating these easy-to-prepare sauces to follow, and that is to use the freshest and best ingredients available.

Here's wishing you an Underwater adventure you will not forget!

Miami Beach Dill Sauce

Dill sauce is simply wonderful on poached or broiled fish and shellfish. Marina Polvay, executive chef and a good friend, gave me this recipe years ago from The Forge restaurant on chic Miami Beach.

1 cup watercress leaves
¹/₄ cup minced scallions
2 tablespoons fresh minced parsley
1 cup mayonnaise
3 anchovy fillets, chopped
3 tablespoons fresh lemon juice to taste
Salt and white pepper to taste
3 to 4 tablespoons minced fresh dill
¹/₂ cup sour cream

1. Place all ingredients, except the dill and sour cream, into the container of blender or food processor. Blend until smooth. Add the dill and blend 1 or 2 seconds, until the dill has just been absorbed.

2. Remove from blender or food processor and whisk in sour cream. Add salt and white pepper to taste. Chill thoroughly before serving.

YIELD: ABOUT 1 ¹/₂ CUPS OF SAUCE
PREPARATION TIME: 10 MINUTES
CHILLING TIME: 1 HOUR OR MORE

THE FORGE, MIAMI BEACH

Seafood Shack Seafood Sauce

This sauce is perfect for crêpes or any fish. If using to stuff crêpes, make the sauce at the last minute. Brush filled, rolled crêpes with a little melted butter, then place under the broiler for a minute or two. It is also scrumptious over steamed Jasmine rice or chopped spinach.

1/4 cup butter
1 small onion, diced
1 cup fresh sliced mushrooms
Roux* (3 tablespoons butter and 3 tablespoons all-purpose flour)
1 1/2 cups milk
4 tablespoons sherry
1/2 pound crab meat, picked over
1/2 pound fish fillets, such as sole, cut in pieces (include only if used
    to stuff crêpes)
1/2 pound scallops, cut in small pieces
1/2 pound shrimp, peeled, deveined, and cut in small pieces
1 teaspoon Worcestershire sauce
1 dash Tabasco sauce
Salt and pepper to taste
2 tablespoons chopped parsley

1. Melt the butter and sauté onions and mushrooms until onions are golden brown. Set aside.

2. Make a roux* with butter and flour and gradually add the milk and then the sherry. Stir constantly until mixture starts to thicken. Add seafood, Worcestershire, Tabasco, salt, and pepper, and cook until seafood is done. Add mushrooms and onions. Sprinkle with parsley.

* SEE GLOSSARY

SERVES: 8 IF FISH SAUCE, 6 FOR CRÊPE STUFFING
PREPARATION TIME: 10 MINUTES
COOKING TIME: APPROXIMATELY 15 MINUTES

VILANO SEAFOOD SHACK, ST. AUGUSTINE

Café Chauveron's Fennel Sauce

André at Café Chauveron suggested using this sauce with fresh, poached salmon. I've tried it on baked and broiled snapper, grouper, and stuffed trout. It's a winner.

1 quart fish stock*
Roux* (3 tablespoons butter and 3 tablespoons all-purpose flour)
1 small bunch of fresh fennel
1 tablespoon butter
2 shallots, chopped
1/4 cup dry white wine
1/2 cup heavy cream
2 egg yolks
Salt and white pepper to taste

1. Add stock to roux* to thicken slightly.

2. Steam the leafy green part of the fennel 2 minutes and add to stock. Simmer 20 minutes.

3. In a separate pan, sauté shallots in butter, add wine and reduce*.

4. Add warmed cream to wine mixture and reduce again. Add this mixture to stock and fennel. Purée and strain.

5. Add egg yolks, one at a time, stirring constantly. Do not boil after adding yolks. Correct for salt and pepper seasoning.

6. Braise bulb of fennel cut in quarters as you would celery or endive. Use fresh lemon juice to keep it white. Use for garnish on whichever dish you prepare.

* SEE GLOSSARY

YIELD: 1 QUART
PREPARATION TIME: 20 MINUTES
COOKING TIME: 30 MINUTES

CAFÉ CHAUVERON, BAY HARBOR ISLAND

O'Steen's Shrimp Sauce

For years O'Steen's has been my initial stop-off when visiting the country's oldest city. The shrimp are grand; fresh, large, and very flavorful. This sauce, famous for years, enhances the shrimp and brings fried shrimp to a whole new level. The sauce's light color is because of the mayonnaise, but don't be deceived—it's VERY tangy!

1 cup mayonnaise
3/4 cup catsup
2 tablespoons Worcestershire sauce
2 tablespoons horseradish
1 tablespoon hot sauce

1. Mix thoroughly, chill, and serve with freshly fried shrimp or other fried seafood.

YIELD: 2 CUPS
PREPARATION TIME: 5 MINUTES

O'STEEN'S, ST. AUGUSTINE

Stone Crab Mustard Sauce

This is the famous sauce for stone crabs, but it can also be used on beef. JoAnn Bass, the granddaughter of the original owner, and a good friend, gave me this recipe nearly 20 years ago. It is a classic in the world of Florida cuisine.

8 tablespoons English mustard
1 quart mayonnaise
1/2 cup steak sauce
1/2 cup Worcestershire sauce
1/2 cup heavy cream

1. In a medium-size bowl, combine the mustard, mayonnaise, steak sauce, and Worcestershire sauce. Using a wire whisk, beat until smooth. Slowly add the cream and continue to beat until you reach proper sauce consistency, thick and creamy. Refrigerate. Serve chilled.

NOTE: Reserve leftover sauce; it will last several days in the refrigerator.

SERVES: 1 1/2 QUARTS
PREPARATION TIME: 5 MINUTES
YIELD: 5 CUPS

JOE'S STONE CRAB RESTAURANT, MIAMI BEACH

Shrimp Sauce in Tarragon Cream

This is a delicious sauce or terrific over steamed rice! If fresh tarragon (that perennial aromatic herb) is not available, use dried, but do not leave it out.

2 tablespoons butter

2 tablespoons all-purpose flour

1 cup heavy cream

1/2 cup bottled clam juice (available in most supermarkets)

1 cup dry white wine such as Chardonnay

1/2 pound cooked "titi" shrimp,** shelled, deveined, and split

2 teaspoons fresh chopped parsley

1/2 teaspoon tarragon

1. Melt butter in heavy pan and stir in flour. Stir over a low heat for 5 minutes. Remove from heat and whisk in cream, clam juice, and wine. Return to heat and stir constantly until sauce thickens.

2. Stir in shrimp, parsley, and tarragon until shrimp are just heated through.

3. Serve over Shrimp Mousse (see recipe, page 87).

** IF "TITI" SHRIMP ARE NOT AVAILABLE, CHOP UP MEDIUM-SIZED SHRIMP FOR SAUCE.

SERVES: 6
PREPARATION TIME: 5 MINUTES
COOKING TIME: 10 TO 15 MINUTES

DERBY LANE RESTAURANT, ST. PETERSBURG

Lobster Sauce Chauveron

This extravaganza lends itself to napping* a mousse beautifully. This recipe is exactly as they made it at Chauveron.

1 1-pound lobster, cleaned
Canola or vegetable oil for sautéing
2 carrots, chopped
1 onion, chopped
1 leek, chopped
3 shallots, chopped
2 celery stalks, chopped
1 head of garlic, chopped
Dry white wine
Dash cognac
1 quart fish stock*
1 cup tomato purée
2 thyme leaves
1 bay leaf
Pinch of tarragon
Salt
1 teaspoon cayenne pepper
Beurre manié* (3/4 cup butter, 3/4 cup flour)
1 quart heavy cream

* SEE GLOSSARY

CONTINUED...

1. Cut tail off lobster and split in half. Chop the head and body in as many small pieces as possible. Crack the claws. Sauté the lobster in hot oil in a large saucepan until very red in color. Add the carrots, onion, leek, shallots, and garlic, and sauté for 10 to 15 minutes.

2. Deglaze* with dry white wine and cognac. Cook for 2 minutes. Add fish stock, tomato purée, and the rest of the seasonings. Bring to a boil and cook 15 minutes. Take out claws and tail and remove meat. Reserve meat.

3. With a slotted spoon, remove the vegetables and the lobster shells from the sauce. Bring the sauce to a boil and add the beurre manié, stirring until the sauce thickens. Strain the sauce.

4. In a separate pan, bring 1 quart of heavy cream to a boil. Add the above lobster sauce to the cream and stir. Chop up the reserved lobster meat and fold into the sauce. Adjust the seasonings.

* SEE GLOSSARY

SERVES: 8
PREPARATION TIME: 1 HOUR
COOKING TIME: 45 TO 60 MINUTES

CAFÉ CHAUVERON, BAY HARBOR ISLAND

Pepin's Orange Mustard Sauce

Of course you will want to use Florida marmalade in this recipe. You can use orange jelly, but the peel and fruit in a marmalade make this recipe one you will not forget. They serve this recipe with Shrimp Almendrina (see recipe, page 104) at Pepin's Restaurant on Fourth Street in my hometown, St. Petersburg. You'll love this distinct flavor.

3/4 cup orange marmalade
1/4 cup chicken or beef stock
2 tablespoons fresh lemon juice
1 teaspoon dry mustard
Few drops hot pepper sauce

1. Combine all ingredients. Chill. Serve on the side for dunking shrimp or other seafood.

YIELD: ABOUT 1 CUP

PEPIN'S, ST. PETERSBURG

Curry Sauce à la Monique

This curry sauce will add the final touch to cooked shell or fin fish. Use a good curry powder such as the Jamaican-style Blue Mountain®, or make your own.

1 cup mayonnaise
1 cup sour cream
1 clove garlic, minced
2 teaspoons curry powder
3 tablespoons extra virgin olive oil
3 tablespoons sugar
Juice of 2 medium oranges, seeded
2 tablespoons fresh lemon juice
2 tablespoons chopped mango chutney
Salt and freshly ground pepper
1 ounce gin

1. Combine mayonnaise and sour cream in a medium mixing bowl and set aside.

2. In a small saucepan or skillet over low heat, sauté garlic and curry powder in extra virgin olive oil until well blended. Remove from heat and stir into mayonnaise-sour cream mixture.

3. Add sugar, orange and lemon juices, chutney, salt, and pepper to taste and bland until smooth. Chill.

4. Just before serving, stir gin into sauce.

SERVES: 8
PREPARATION TIME: 15 MINUTES
COOKING TIME: 5 MINUTES
CHILL

THE WINE CELLAR, NORTH REDINGTON BEACH

Simple Tartar Sauce

I have visited Julia Mae's in the Florida panhandle for more than 20 years. Julia made pies very well, but her Tartar Sauce was a winner, too. Here's a good old standby...thin out with vinegar if too thick.

1 tablespoon chopped sweet onions
1 cup mayonnaise
1 tablespoon dill pickle, chopped
1/2 teaspoon granulated garlic

1. Mix ingredients well. Chill.

YIELD: 1 CUP
PREPARATION TIME: 5 MINUTES

JULIA MAE'S, CARRABELLE

Julia Mae's Cocktail Sauce

Decrease hot sauce if necessary-this has a nice zing! A good basic cocktail sauce for use on shrimp, fish and crab cakes, too. I like hot Tabasco sauce, but any will do.

1 cup catsup, or substitute chili sauce
1 tablespoon horseradish
1 teaspoon hot sauce
1/2 teaspoon fresh lemon or lime juice

1. Mix ingredients well. Chill.

YIELD: 1 CUP
PREPARATION TIME: 5 MINUTES

JULIA MAE'S, CARRABELLE

Tempura Sauce (Ten-Tsuyu)

Easy to make, great dipping. Have a lovely meal.

¹/₄ cup chicken stock, or substitute broth
2 teaspoons mirin (sweet sake)
¹/₄ cup shoyu (soy sauce)
¹/₂ teaspoon fresh ginger, peeled and chopped fine
White radish, grated

1. Add mirin, shoyu, and ginger to chicken stock.

2. Garnish with grated white radish. Serve in small bowl for dipping.

YIELD: ¹/₂ CUP
PREPARATION TIME: 5 MINUTES

KYUSHU RESTAURANT-SUSHI BAR, KEY WEST

Mustard Fruit Sauce

This is delicious with tempura shrimp.

1 cup mustard fruits, chopped, available in gourmet specialty shops
1 cup apricot preserves
2 teaspoons Dijon mustard

1. Blend all ingredients in the container of a blender or food processor into a coarse sauce. Do not purée or liquefy.

2. Chill. Serve cold or at room temperature.

YIELD: 2 CUPS
PREPARATION TIME: 2 MINUTES
CHILL

MARTY'S STEAKS, TAMPA

Glossary of Terms

AL DENTE
Literally means "to the tooth" in Italian. The food, particularly pasta, is just barely cooked.

ALL-PURPOSE FLOUR
Plain flour that has no salt or baking powder added.

BÉARNAISE SAUCE
A basic sauce for fish; it is also good on broiled red meat and eggs.
There are two methods.

BLENDER
4 egg yolks
1/2 teaspoon salt
1/8 teaspoon cayenne pepper
1 cup butter, melted
2 tablespoons lemon juice
2 teaspoons minced onion
2 teaspoons minced parsley
2 teaspoons fresh tarragon or 1 teaspoon dried

1. With blender or food processor, beat yolks until thick. Add salt and cayenne.

2. Add melted butter a little at a time, beating constantly.

3. Add remaining ingredients and beat well. Serve while warm.
   Yields about 1 1/2 cups.

CLASSIC
To 3/4 cup hollandaise sauce (see recipe in Glossary), add 1 tablespoon tarragon vinegar and 1 teaspoon each fresh chopped parsley, tarragon, and chervil.

BÉCHAMEL SAUCE
A basic sauce that serves as a base for many classic sauces.

1. Make a roux with 1 tablespoon each of butter and flour. Cook for 2 minutes.

2. Gradually whisk in 3/4 cup milk and 1/4 cup fish stock (see Glossary) or all milk. Whisk until smooth.

3. Cook over low heat until milk is warmed through. Taste for seasoning. Makes about 1 cup.

BEURRE MANIÉ
Used for thickening soups and sauces. Mix 1 teaspoon each of flour and butter (or equal amounts of both). Rub with the heel of your hand until blended and form into a ball or balls. Can be frozen.

BLANCH
Plunge food into boiling water for 30 to 60 seconds, then put under cold running water to stop the cooking process.

BORDELAISE SAUCE
A sauce made from brown sauce or Sauce Espagnole by adding red wine.

2 tablespoons shallots, minced
2 tablespoons butter
3/4 cup red wine
1 1/2 cups brown sauce or canned brown gravy
2 tablespoons lemon juice
2 tablespoons parsley, minced
Salt and pepper to taste
Mushroom, sliced (optional)

1. Sauté shallots in butter until transparent.

2. Add wine and simmer until reduced by half.

3. Add remaining ingredients and heat.

BRAISE
Cook slowly in fat until brown, then add a small amount of liquid, covering and simmering.

BROWN SAUCE/SAUCE ESPAGNOLE (QUICK)

A rich beef stock reduced and thickened with roux. (See glossary for directions)
May be purchased as beef gravy.

To make brown sauce:
1. Melt 2 tablespoons butter.

2. Stir in 1/2 clove of garlic and remove after 10 seconds.

3. Stir in 2 tablespoons flour to make a roux.

4. Cook 2 minutes.

5. Whisk in 1 cup canned beef bouillon or broth.

6. Continue whisking until broth comes to a boil.

7. Season to taste.

BUTTERFLY
Cut against the grain or cut lengthwise, leaving flesh attached on one side.
This is done for appearance and to tenderize.

CARMELIZE
Melt sugar until it is liquid and light brown.

CHOP
Separate into small pieces, about 1/4-inch cubes. The sharper the knife, the
easier it is to do.

CLAM STOCK
Strain liquid remaining after steaming clams open. Bottled clam juice can be used
instead, but reduce the amount of salt called for in recipe.

CLARIFIED BUTTER
Make butter clear by heating and removing all whey and sediment as it rises
to the top.

1. Slowly heat butter until completely melted.

2. Carefully skim off the whey (white matter) that rises to the top. The remaining
clear (clarified) butter keeps for at least a week if tightly covered and refrigerated.

COURT-BOUILLON
A highly seasoned fish broth.

Trimmings (bones, head, tail, etc.) from fish
1 onion stuck with cloves
1 carrot, 1 celery stalk, cut in thirds
4 to 5 sprigs parsley
2 cups water
1 cup white wine

1. Simmer for 20 minutes.

2. Strain and taste for seasonings.

If using for shellfish recipe, replace fish trimmings with appropriate shells from lobster, crab, etc. In a pinch, use bottled clam juice.

CRACKER MEAL
Fine meal made from crackers, finer than cornmeal and used as a more delicate coating for meats. Can be made from unsalted soda crackers rolled on a wooden board with a rolling pan.

CREAM SAUCE
Béchamel sauce made with cream instead of milk.

CRÈME FRAÎCHE
To make this slightly soured cream, add 1 tablespoon buttermilk to 1 cup heavy cream. Let sit in warm place overnight, or about 8 to 12 hours, until thick.

CRÊPES
Thin pancakes (use blender or food processor).

3 to 4 eggs
1 cup flour
1 1/2 cups milk
1/2 teaspoon salt
3 tablespoons butter, melted

1. Combine all ingredients in processor and blend until smooth. Allow batter to rest 1 hour before frying. May be kept in refrigerator for 1 week.

2. Pour 2 tablespoons of mixture into 6-inch pan to make a single crêpe.

DEEP FRY
Cook by immersing in hot oil or fat in a pan deep enough for oil to cover food completely.

DEGLAZE
Use a liquid (water, broth, or wine) to "clean" a cooking pan. Turn heat under pan to high, add required liquid, and use a wooden spoon to scrape up particles used in sauce.

DEMI-GLACÉ
A rich brown sauce that's slowly cooked until it's reduced to a thick glaze that coats a spoon.

DEVEIN
Clean shrimp by removing black filament from the back, before or after cooking.

DICE
Cut into small cubes, usually about an eighth of an inch square.

DREDGE IN, DUST WITH FLOUR
Dip meat in or sprinkle lightly with flour.

FATBACK
Pure pork fat that is cut from the back of the pig, fresh or salt-cured.

FILLET
Boneless meat or fish. Cut or slice fish that has been cleaned, deheaded, and scaled down both sides of the backbone.

FISH STOCK
See court-bouillon. (See page 268)

FLAMBÉ (FLAME)
Cover food lightly with spirits and carefully ignite. It is to add flavor or beauty when serving.

FOLD

Mix one ingredient into another slowly and gently, without breaking, as with egg whites that must be kept light and fluffy.

GARLIC BUTTER

Mash 4 to 6 cloves garlic and mince. Work into 1 stick softened butter. Refrigerate and use as needed.

GLAZE

A thin, smooth coating such as milk, melted butter, or other ingredient brushed on top of food to give it a shiny appearance.

HOLLANDAISE SAUCE (BLENDER)

3 egg yolks
2 teaspoons lemon juice
1/4 teaspoon salt
Dash of cayenne
1/2 cup butter, melted

1. In blender or food processor, beat yolks until thickened. Beat in juice, salt, and cayenne.

2. Pour hot butter in a stream with machine running. Serve in warmed bowl. Yields 1 cup.

HOLLANDAISE SAUCE (CLASSIC)

3/4 cup butter, melted
3 egg yolks, beaten
4 teaspoons lemon juice
Dash of salt and cayenne

1. In top of double boiler, melt 1/3 of the butter. Beat in eggs and juice with wire whisk.

2. Add remaining butter slowly, beating constantly until mixture thickens—never allowing water to boil.

3. Stir in seasonings and serve. Yields 3/4 cup.

JULIENNE
Cut into thin strips or matchlike sticks with a very sharp knife.

KNEAD
Work a mass of dough into a uniform texture by folding and pressing with the heels of your hands until dough is smooth and elastic.

MARINATE
Soak food in liquid usually pickled with vinegar or wine and oil, as well as spices and herbs that both add flavor and tenderize the meat or fish. The liquid is called marinade.

MINCE
Chop into very tiny pieces.

MOUSSELINE SAUCE
Add half a cup of whipped cream to 1 cup hollandaise sauce (See page 270) just before serving.

NAP
Coat food with thin, even layer of sauce.

PERNOD
A yellowish, licorice-flavored liqueur similar to absinthe. It is very popular in France, where it is often served with water. Pernod also is similar to anisette, a clear, sweet liqueur that tastes like licorice.

POACH
Cook food gently in liquid that is barely simmering.

PUREE
Force food through a sieve or blend in food processor until smooth.

REDUCE
Boil or simmer a liquid until it is less; to concentrate flavor.

ROUX (BROWN AND WHITE)

Used as a base for many sauces.

Melt butter and stir in flour (recipes usually call for equal amounts of both). Cook, stirring constantly for several minutes, until golden or brown as recipe indicates.

SALT PORK

Generally pork fat cured in salt.

SAUCE ESPAGNOLE

See brown sauce. (See page 267)

SAUTÉ

Cook in a shallow pan, in a small amount of butter or fat. Brown evenly to seal in the juices.

SCORE

Make shallow cuts in the surface of meat.

SIMMER

Cook in water or other liquid below or just at the boiling point.

STEAM

Expose to water vapor by cooking with a small amount of boiling water in a tightly covered pan.

SWEAT

Let drops of moisture form on the surface of food. Usually done in pan over low heat with buttered wax paper covering food and topped with the pan lid. This helps to intensify flavor.

VEAL STOCK (SAUCE)

4 veal bones, rinsed and cracked
1 carrot, peeled and chopped
1 onion, chopped
3 stalks celery, chopped
Several parsley sprigs
1 bay leaf
6 whole cloves, slightly bruised
¹/₄ teaspoon thyme

1. Simmer for several hours.

2. Strain, taste for seasoning, and cool.

VELOUTÉ SAUCE

Use fish stock as part of the liquid when making béchamel sauce.

VIN ROUGE

Add red wine to fish velouté sauce.

ZEST

The peel (not the white pith) part of citrus fruit that is grated and often poached or candied. Used as a flavor enhancer or for garnish.

Category Index

LUNCHEON DISHES OR LATE SUPPERS

Lobster Lover

Alphabetical Index

D

E

F

M

N

O

S